KUMU HULA:
CHALLENGING JOURNEY
OF A HULA MASTER

Minoru Yanagihashi
and
Leiola Aquino Galla

XULON PRESS

Xulon Press
2301 Lucien Way #415
Maitland, FL 32751
407.339.4217
www.xulonpress.com

© 2019 by MINORU YANAGIHASHI AND LEIOLA AQUINO GALLA

All rights reserved solely by the author. The author guarantees all contents are original and do not infringe upon the legal rights of any other person or work. No part of this book may be reproduced in any form without the permission of the author. The views expressed in this book are not necessarily those of the publisher.

Unless otherwise indicated, Scripture quotations are taken from:

The King James Version. Public domain.

The Holy Bible, New International Version®, NIV® Copyright © 1973, 1978, 1984, 2011 by Biblica, Inc.® Used by permission. All rights reserved worldwide.

Printed in the United States of America.

ISBN-13: 978-1-5456-8115-2

CONTENTS

PREFACE vii
ACKNOWLEDGMENTS xiii

CHAPTER ONE   The Halau 15
CHAPTER TWO   Kumu Hula 29
CHAPTER THREE   Development of Hula 41
CHAPTER FOUR   Hawaiian Renaissance and Hula 55
CHAPTER FIVE   Formative Years 71
CHAPTER SIX   Fulfilling the Task 99
CHAPTER SEVEN   Christian Hula and Globalization 115
CHAPTER EIGHT   Therapeutic Hula 131

EPILOGUE 145
GLOSSARY 157
BIBLIOGRAPHY 163

PREFACE

Few books and articles have dealt with the kumu hula (hula master). As hula became a ceremonial dance and began to be taught by highly skilled individuals, these teachers were recognized as masters of the hula. The title *kumu hula*, however, was not widely used until the 1960s. Considering the long history of the hula, this is a relatively recent development. The increasing popularity of the hula led to the emergence of many new kumu hula. To some critics, the title of kumu hula was tarnished by this sudden inclusion. How can the venerated title, whose reputation was built by pioneer teachers, be maintained if not enhanced? This question is partly answered by the journey of a kumu hula. We learn of the background of hula, the demanding terrain covered, and the vision for hula arising from new territories explored. This journey is a microcosm of the world of hula, a story to be added to by other fellow travelers.

There is no legal procedure to becoming a kumu hula. It is a form of recognition developed within the hula community and was formalized during the renaissance of Hawaiian culture and the revival of hula in the 1970s. The acceptance of certain roles and functions of a teacher of the hula and the successful carrying out of these responsibilities became necessary steps leading to the title of kumu hula. There is a recognition ceremony, the formal *'uniki* (graduation exercise) that is accepted as the ritual ceremony, signifying the attainment of kumu hula. Nevertheless, there are several kumu hula who have not gone through the *'uniki* ceremony but are just as effective as those who have. It seems, to be successful as a kumu hula, one does not have to go through *'uniki,* or hold a certificate, but all that is necessary is to be able to carry out the essential three-fold tasks of learning from your past kumu, transmitting this knowledge and skills to present students, and training disciples to pass the knowledge and skills to future generations. Still, the title is necessary because it helps to command respect, which is essential to being a successful teacher. The proliferation of titles continues to evoke prolonged discussion as to what constitutes a kumu hula and his or her roles and responsibilities.

In going over the biographical sketches of several kumu, a few characteristics stand out. First, most kumu were born into or were exposed to Hawaiian culture at an early age. They grew up in families where Hawaiian culture was appreciated, and where Hawaiian was spoken. Fluency in the language was not needed, but sheer exposure was a great advantage. Second, they usually underwent a long period of training and study and were under the tutelage of a principal kumu and were influenced by other kumu. Finally, they all possessed a deep love, passion, and commitment to hula. They loved to share their knowledge and experience with students, close associates, family, and relatives. However, they were reluctant to share their stories with the general public. This inward-looking attitude kept their views and activities within the confines of the halau (meeting place). The activities were considered private and remained within the hula family. They were further constrained by strict halau rules.

Leiola Aquino Galla was approached and asked several times to tell her story, but she did not feel confident and always felt the time was not right. "To every thing there is a season, and a time to every purpose under the heaven" (Ecclesiastes 3:1 KJV).

At long last, on the thirteenth inquiry, she decided the time was right. One of the tragedies of life is too many go to their graves with their songs or messages still trapped within their hearts, crying to get out. It is never too late to share! Furthermore, there comes a time when there is a need to acknowledge the knowledge and skills acquired from kumu and the kindness and support received from them. Even if they have passed from the scene, there is a need to acknowledge this debt. Finally, with advancement of age, the question of legacy becomes important. There comes a time of reflection on what lasting impressions one made. What messages or contributions could be left with students and other followers and with the hula community? The time has come to finally share.

The role of the kumu is best understood when the activities within the halau are examined. Each kumu has his or her distinctive style and priorities. Critical decisions have to be made, whether to emphasize *kahiko* (ancient hula) or *'auana* (modern hula), or a combination of both. How much innovation should be allowed? Should the purity of traditional hula be strictly maintained? How about other Polynesian dances, for example, Tahitian, Samoan, and Maori? Can there be a satisfying balance? And then, there is the question of entering hula contests, and how much attention should be placed on this pursuit.

Over the years, broad forces twice threatened hula. The first threat came from missionaries and their adherents and was based on religious and moral grounds. Hula survived by being practiced privately and in secrecy. The second threat was more insidious and could be called the "Americanization of hula." Hula was bastardized and became pure entertainment—it was commercialized and became flashy, glamorous, and devoid of substance. In the historical chapters on the development of hula and its renaissance, we describe the threats and the resulting development of modern hula and its variant forms. Leiola Aquino

Galla's journey takes place within this background of the decline and then the revival of hula.

Another area of controversy is whether hula can be applied in a different cultural environment. Can hula be considered a dance form that transcends Hawaiian culture and religion? Can it be exported to other countries, and can it be used in a Christian context? Hula emerged out of the ancient Hawaiian religion with its beliefs, myths, and rituals and was condemned by the missionaries, but it survived, in part, in a modified form that incorporated Western influences. Critics bemoan the loss of authenticity when hula is exported or when it is used in another religion. But change was inevitable if hula was to survive. Globalization of hula is taking place, and hula is flourishing in diverse cultural surroundings. This is the reality—globalization and Christian hula will continue to flourish. The challenge is to protect and preserve the old dance forms and chants in the midst of all the changes. Through this journey, we see Leiola Aquino Galla's love for hula, her enthusiasm for the changes taking place, especially for Christian hula, and her commitment not to forget the ancient dances. Hula is the artistic language of Hawai'i, but hula is also the artistic language of the whole world.

In this joint effort, one collaborator brings the inner perspective of a long-time dancer and expert teacher of hula, while the other collaborator brings the detached, fresh viewpoint of a nonparticipant, an outsider. It is hoped a complete inside-outside perspective can be achieved—an inside view of what is taking place in hula and an outside view of its role in the wider communities. Both collaborators are natives of Hawai'i, and in fact, went to the same high school, although at different times. They are both students of Hawaiian culture and share a common love for the culture. Therefore, the product you will be reading is the result of corporate authorship and with it comes joint responsibility. This work is intended for the general reader, but hula devotees should find it informative and inspiring. This has been our goal.

A note on the use of Hawaiian words is needed. There are no plurals for nouns in the Hawaiian language, so the plural "s" is not used. However, words, such as *lei* and *lu'au,* have become part of the English language and are treated as English words with the plural "s." Hawaiian words have been italicized but not place and proper names. Frequently used words, such as halau, kumu, and hula (by itself) are not italicized. The diacritical mark known as *'okina* (glottal stop) is shown as ('); it is used because its omission would change the meaning of the word. However, the *kahako* (macron), a diacritical mark placed above a vowel as an aid to proper pronunciation by indicating a stressed and elongated vowel, has been omitted. This may bother linguists and other specialists, but for the general reader, it should not be troublesome. Diacritical marks used are in accordance with usage or are based on Pukui and Elbert's *Hawaiian Dictionary* (1986). A glossary of Hawaiian words used in the text is appended.

ACKNOWLEDGMENTS

Leiola expresses her gratitude for her parents' patience and loving support during the formative period of her career as a dancer and teacher. She is indebted to the kumu with whom she was closely associated and is thankful for the sharing of their knowledge and skills.

We appreciate the inputs of the advanced students. Their contributions greatly enhanced the discussion of Leiola as a teacher.

We are grateful for the use of the photographs of the kumu derived from the Kalihi-Palama Cultural and Arts Society, and we acknowledge the use of photographs taken by the renown photographer, Boone Morrison.

Finally, we extend our thanks to Mark Yanagihashi for his help in data and image management.

CHAPTER ONE

THE HALAU

"'A'ohe pau ka 'ike i ka halau ho'okahi."
("All knowledge is not taught in the same school.")
Hawaiian proverb[1]

On the eastern border of downtown Tucson, along Kino Highway and just south of the campus of the University of Arizona, lie several rows of office/warehouse–type buildings. On the window of one of the nondescript offices is a sign "Leiola Hula Halau."[2] Entering this office, the room is a typical office space, but instead of the usual desks, chairs, and filing cabinets, there are Hawaiian garments hanging on racks and bolts of bright Hawaiian print fabric lying on shelves. A couple of counters displaying handmade Polynesian crafts and trinkets are arranged around the room. A short hallway leads to the back, and on the right of the hallway is a large walk-in closet space with *mu'umu'u*

---

[1] The Hawaiian proverbs quoted in this book are from: Mary Kawena Pukui, *'Olelo No'eau: Hawaiian Proverbs and Poetical Sayings* (Honolulu: Bishop Museum Press, 1983).

[2] *Halau* is a meeting place where hula is taught. Also, the word is used to denote a hula group meeting at this specific place.

hanging in the racks.[3] On the left side of the hallway, there is a kitchenette with a sink, a small refrigerator, cabinets, and a counter, but no stove. The hallway leads to a large back room with floor inlaid with wood veneer. A large mirror covers most of the right wall, and the opposite wall has an unusual decoration—a small canoe! On the left side floor are various musical instruments, including *ipu* (gourd), *ipu heke* (double gourd), *'uli 'uli* (feathered gourd rattle), *pu'ili* (split-bamboo rattle), *pahu* (drum), *'ili 'ili* (pebbles), and *kala'au* (rhythm sticks).

Tucson halau

Of all the decorations, the most intriguing are photographs posted all around the room. There are pictures of dancers taken many years ago at lu'aus, parties, hula recitals, and other special events. Some are faded and turning brown but still visibly conveying the tradition and legacy of the halau. In the movie *Dead Poets Society* (1989), Robin Williams portrays a prep school

---

[3] *Mu'umu'u* is a loose-fitting gown.

teacher. In one scene, he gathers his students around a showcase displaying championship trophies and an old photograph of a baseball team. He asks his students to move in closer and examine the old picture. Soon their noses are pressed against the glass showcase. "If you listen real close, you can hear them whisper their legacy to you. Can't you hear what they are saying? Go on, lean in and listen. You hear it . . . *carpe diem*" (which is Latin for "seize the day"). It is the message the students of long ago are sharing with the current boys—that they should make the most of their opportunities.

Tucson halau

Similarly, the photographs in the halau are speaking to the hula students. Now, look at this old, faded photo of four long-gone dancers—look at their radiant, smiling faces. Can't you sense their excitement and enjoyment? Press in closer and listen—ah, you can hear them saying softly, *"E hula mai kakou"* ("come dance with us"). This is the mantra of the halau. Former students are inviting you to join in the dance!

The *haumana* (students) begin to arrive. They are properly dressed, for there is a strict dress code; for example, women are required to wear undergarments. The students have with them their hula bag with the requisite pen or pencil and notebook. The *haumana* enter the room with reverence. It is the same kind of respect martial arts students extend when entering the *dojo* (exercise room). There is no rushing in and horsing around; instead, they enter quietly, take off their shoes, and neatly arrange them near the entrance. Then they greet the kumu hula, Leiola Aquino Galla, and proceed to their sitting spot, sitting down on the floor with their legs crossed or sitting on the back of their legs, Japanese style. There are absolutely no chairs in the room; it is completely bare of furniture.

The *haumana* are called to form a prayer circle, holding hands. Kumu Leiola asks if someone would like to give the opening prayer. A student volunteers and prayer requests are taken before the prayer is offered. The *haumana* then forms two lines facing the mirrored wall with the *'alaka'i* (teaching assistant) at the front, and in the center, all face the kumu hula who is at the front. No talking or even whispering is allowed and, of course, no cell phone.

After the kumu hula makes some announcements, a ten-to-fifteen minute warm-up exercise begins to properly prepare the students' bodies for the practice session. The exercise music emanating from a CD player is a Christian hula chanted and accompanied by the beat of the *ipu* (bottle gourd), thus providing the rhythm and controlling the tempo.[4] According to Kumu Leiola, "Christian hula is ideal for the warm-up, for its graceful movements relieve stress."

---

[4] The *'uli 'uli* (featured gourd rattle) is sometimes used for this purpose.

Another CD is inserted into the player, and Hawaiian music softly wafts through the room. The formal instruction begins; it is a one-and-a-half-hour long session. Kumu Leiola prefers to start with Christian hula, followed by *kahiko* (ancient dances) and *'auana* (modern dances). She does not interrupt the dance to make corrections. Corrections and instructions are made during the break between dances, and the *haumana,* at that moment, take notes and record them in their notebook. In the old days, note taking was not allowed, and all instructions had to be memorized. There were no manuals, outlines, or any other printed materials.

Over the years, however, kumu learned that with the younger generation, the taking of notes was essential; it focused attention and expedited learning.[5] Kumu Leiola says, "It is an absolute must—students have to bring their notepads and must take notes. If they have their own small instruments, they are asked to bring them." With the advance in technology, even the pen and notepad have been replaced by iPad and iPhone. The final set of lessons concludes, and the class session ends with a Christian hula.

The students are Caucasian women, ranging in age from their early twenties to middle age. They are from various background, including housewives, retirees, office workers, professionals, and college students. Male students, by the way, are rare. "Occasionally, there are Asian women, but Pacific Islanders are rare," says Kumu Leiola. If a person from Hawai'i should attend, she says it would affect the tenor of the group. Filipino and Japanese, she says, tend to be exceptional, being motivated and having strong work ethics.

---

[5] Ma'iki Aiu Lake was one of the first to use a blackboard and required note taking. She was criticized for doing it.

What is provided above is a snapshot of the Leiola Hula Halau. The halau is neither large nor fancy but probably representative of what one would find in a halau. There is no denying halau could vary widely. They could vary by size, type of facility, equipment, program, and most critically in the personnel, especially the founder and leader, the kumu hula. Some have a long history and tradition. One of the oldest and most prestigious is Halau O Kekuhi, the halau of the Kanaka'ole family on the Big Island. Today, it is led by Nalani Kanaka'ole and Huihui Kanahele-Mossman, the family leaders dating back seven generations. The halau is reputed to be the "guardian of the treasury of Pele chants and dances." Despite the long history and the many diverse groups, there is no governing body to bring them together. There is no national association of halau, and no authoritative and coordinating body to police and regulate the halau. They are independent of each other.

Kanaka'ole family
L to R: Pualani Kanahele (daughter); Edith (mother)
Nalani (daughter)

As to the number of halau, although the figures are somewhat imprecise, one can make a reasonable estimate. The number is impressive with over 1,100 halau throughout the world![6] Over 850 (80%) are in the United States, and about 250 are international (see Table 1). As expected, Hawai'i has the highest concentration with 243 halau, and within the city limits of Honolulu, there are thirty-nine halau. This is a large number for such a limited geographical space. Kumu Leiola says, "If she returns to Hawai'i, she wouldn't want to add to the number of halau."

---

[6] The figures given are based on reports submitted to mele.com. Only halau reporting to mele.com are listed. Nevertheless, the data give a reasonable picture of the number of halau and their location.

TABLE 1

Number of Halau in Selected Locations

United States		Foreign Countries	
Hawai'i	234	Mexico	117
California	221	Japan	46
Washington	53	Canada	23
Texas	42		
Florida	28		
Arizona	23		
Nevada	23		

Source: mele.com (2018)

Many natives of Hawai'i migrated to California, especially to the Bay Area and to Los Angeles. A few migrants had a deep love for Hawaiian culture and missed dancing the hula and wanted to share it with others. Their background varied—some were born and raised in Hawai'i, others were former long-term visitors and students, or those who had worked for an extended period in Hawai'i. They had trained under a primary kumu, had been influenced by other kumu, and had achieved proficiency in the dances. To give just two examples of prominent halau in the Bay Area, there is Na Lei Hulu I Ka Wekiu, led by pioneer Kumu Patrick Makuakane in San Francisco, and the Academy of Hawaiian Arts of iconic Kumu Mark Keali'i Ho'omalu in Hayward, across the bay from San Francisco. Both are huge and long-established halau that have put on lavish stage productions, often fund-raising events, and have sold out venues with 6,000 seats![7]

But most halau are not large and are not involved in large fund-raising projects. If funds are needed to enter a competition, for an excursion, or for any extracurricular activities, small-scale fund-raisers are used, such as bake sales, T-shirt sales, and so forth. For most, the primary reason for establishing the halau was just the enjoyment of participating in and teaching hula. Some kumu enjoyed working with *keiki* (children) and found the enthusiasm of the children and their potential personally rewarding. If money was made teaching and performing, it was all for the good, but making money was not the sole purpose. Many halau are nonprofit organizations, but Leiola Hula Halau is a for-profit organization; Kumu Leiola wanted to avoid the many restrictions imposed by Internal Revenue Service on nonprofits. It is not difficult to set up a halau, for there are only a few legal requirements and government regulations.

---

[7] Liza Simon, "A Tale of Two Kumu," *Hana Hou!* 14, no. 1 (February/March 2011): 48–59.

Two things are required to establish a halau: students and a space large enough to accommodate and train them. On the first, the best approach in recruiting students is the time-honored word of mouth. "I believe in going out into the community, being involved in activities, and making known the halau," says Kumu Leiola. It is the best way to make contacts and to spread the word. Since advertisement can be expensive, free sources of publicity are sought, such as announcements in small community papers, listing in cultural events calendars, posting fliers on public bulletin boards, and placing fliers in business establishments. With the advent of technology, websites have become the most inexpensive and effective way to attract students and required little time commitment. Social media plays a major role in attracting the younger generation. It is an open market with many halau adopting the Hawaiian proverb, "*A'ohe pau ka 'ike i ka halau ho'okahi*" ("All knowledge is not found under one roof"). This has become the mantra for many halau. There is no monopoly of knowledge and talent in the world of hula.

Many students are referred to a halau, and their attendance depends largely on the reputation and preeminence of the kumu hula. What does the halau have to offer? What are its emphases, priorities, styles, methods of teaching, and specializations? The amount of focus placed on *hula kahiko* or on *hula 'auana* is an important distinction. Each halau has a trademark or distinctive style—they are not alike. The Kanaka'ole family halau on the Big Island, for example, is famous for its *'aiha'a* style of hula with its bended knees, low-posture steps done in a vigorous fashion, mimicking the volcanic eruptions, forcefully coming up from the ground. Kumu Leiola says, "I can tell what halau the dancers are from by their foot and hand movements." For those with trained eyes, they can easily detect the differences in style.

Finding a suitable space could be a challenge because of the financial constraints. If possible, free space is sought or one with a minimum fee. An immediate solution is to use a part of the kumu's home—it could be the garage, living room, or lanai. A public facility would be another choice. If a school district is accommodating, a school cafeteria could be used. Being larger than a classroom, it would have an adequate dancing area without moving furniture. In Hawai'i, the school cafeteria is an option commonly chosen. A church auditorium is another possibility. In Eugene, Oregon, Kumu Leiola initially used a public library basement room as her halau, and it turned out to be a success. Generally speaking, however, it is difficult to find a public facility willing to block out a convenient time slot for an extended period. Occasionally, a community facility is available through the parks and recreation department of the city. Even an outdoor park area has been used, at least temporarily until a room could be found.

Another alternative would be a room used for exercise purposes. When Kumu Leiola moved to Tucson, she initially resorted to spas and gyms; in fact, she used a total of seven over the years. While it is common for kumu to move their halau, it is still a disruptive process. "Finally, I was able to get away from the spas and gyms and move into a better facility. It had 600 square feet of floor space with an outside restroom. At first, the rent was $600 per month, but unfortunately, rent was increased every year, and this went on for five years," Kumu Leiola says. She then started using fitness centers, but they too had a disadvantage. "The owners gave only 'junk time,' for example, from 3:00 to 4:00 p.m. when the facility was fairly empty," says Kumu Leiola. These were simply bad times for everyone concerned.

"More limiting as to the type of clients allowed were the senior centers at retirement communities; otherwise, they did work out rather well," says Kumu Leiola. "The clients had to be residents of the retirement community, and outsiders were not allowed." Kumu Leiola did not limit herself to the Tucson city limits and was willing to drive outside of Tucson within reasonable distances. Retirement community senior centers tended to be outside the city limits. There are no easy solutions to finding a suitable dancing facility, and since few kumu have the financial resources to own their own buildings, it meant a constant search for a better and convenient rental space, but rarely was there a perfect fit.

The following is a summary list of locations used by Leiola Hula Halau over a period of a little over twenty years in Tucson. It illustrates how often a kumu has to move the halau and the variety of facilities used. The office/warehouse building was the best place and was rented for seven years.

- Kumu's residence/garage
- Recreation room of apartment complex
- Auditorium of churches (2 churches)
- School cafeteria/auditorium/gym (4 sites)
- Senior centers (3 sites)
- Nonprofit service organizations (2 sites)
- Private ballroom
- Government employment program facility
- Spa and fitness centers (2 sites)
- Office/warehouse building

The logistical challenges are always there, but the efforts to overcome them seem worthwhile when the larger purposes are considered. The halau is more than a dance studio; it is a repository of Hawaiian culture and tradition. Almost all halau have Hawaiian names with symbolic meanings. The halau has a lineage and history and becomes a reference point in a genealogy line. Certain genealogical lines of kumu are recognized for their specialized skills, and some are considered a sort of "cultural treasure." For example, there are a few remaining masters of the ancient forms and styles of *oli* (chanting), *pa'i* (beating or drumming) of percussion instruments, and the translating of chants and old *mele* (songs and poetry). There are experts on the rituals and ancient rules.

The masters offer workshops, imparting specialized knowledge and skills, that are in demand. The translation and cataloging of chants are an ongoing task. Whenever possible, research and preservation continues on ancient footsteps and hand motions. Another activity in the preservation and transmission of Hawaiian culture is the making and use of percussion instruments. Occasionally, Kumu Leiola teaches how to make them. The procedure and techniques are passed on, and there is a practical side—it saves money, since some of the instruments can be a costly expense for the students. Also the risk of receiving instruments damaged in shipping is avoided by making your own.

Besides the instruments, the art of adornment, making feather leis, necklaces, bracelets, and anklets, needs to be continually taught, so the techniques will not be lost. Underlying the activities, are the study and teaching of the Hawaiian language. The halau is not a language school, but a considerable amount of time is spent on research, translation, and teaching of the meaning of words as they pertain to specific songs and chants. Therefore, through all of these activities, the halau helps to preserve and promote Hawaiian culture and tradition.

CHAPTER TWO

KUMU HULA

We've preserved this for many generations, teaching this hula to everybody and all of the many generations of people that have come after us. (Pualani Kanaka'ole Kanahele)

The founder of the halau is known simply as "kumu" or formally as "kumu hula," the master teacher of hula. In the political world, the top leader is recognized and followed because of his or her coercive power obtained by winning political and/or military struggles or because of his or her constitutional or legal authority won by the electoral process. But in the artistic world, the recognition or acceptance of the leader is based on his or her mastery of the art form and for successfully assuming the responsibilities that come with it. He or she is entrusted with the preservation and continuation of Hawaiian culture and traditions, particularly as they pertain to its dance and music. He or she is the translator and interpreter of the Hawaiian language, transforming the words, poetry, and stories into choreographed dance movements. Each kumu has been tutored by kumu, has been influenced by other kumu, and has passed on the accumulated knowledge and skills to others while developing their own unique style. Although the kumu receives the official recognition and personal blessings of his or her primary kumu, the recognition of peers is essential, and it is a respect that has to be earned and is not automatically given. This respect is achieved by responsibly carrying out the role and function of the kumu.

The process of becoming a kumu hula requires the achievement of certain levels of accomplishments. The steps of recognition and promotion and how they are done differ with the kumu and with the halau. In general, the first recognized level is *olapa* (dancer), who only dances and uses small instruments; then comes the *ho'opa'a* (greater experienced and mature dancer), who does the chanting and drumming with larger instruments and takes the lead in songs and utters the refrains.[8] The most senior dancer is the *'alaka'i*, the teaching assistant, who is at the front and center of the group, and takes over the class when the kumu is absent. These positions are recognition of the individual's mastery of skills and of their devotion to hula. Certain protocols have been formalized for the student ready to be kumu hula. Much of this came about when Kumu Ma'ika Aiu Lake formed a special class for potential kumu hula in 1970. The class had to undergo rigorous training and study, and in the end, the class of 1972–73 graduated twenty-eight kumu hula! She set the pace for turning out entire classes of kumu. Previously, kumu had only one or two kumu candidates under their wing; there was no such thing as a "class" of kumu. Nevertheless, huge classes of kumu are rare. There was another large class in 2007 when Halau O Kekuhi of the Kanaka'ole family graduated fourteen kumu hula.

---

[8] Nathaniel B. Emerson, *Unwritten Literature of Hawaii: The Sacred Songs of the Hula* (Rutland: Charles E. Tuttle, 1965), 28.

The elements of the graduation ceremony called *'uniki* vary from kumu to kumu and from halau to halau.[9] However, there are some common features, such as intensive practice sessions, fasting, ritual cleansing in the ocean, and *'ailolo* (ceremonial meal). The *'ailolo* itself is observed in various ways, and one extreme practice is for the student to eat the head, especially the brain, of a fish, dog, or pig that had been offered to the gods and goddesses. Especially coveted is the brain of a black pig. Being a Christian, Kumu Leiola abstained from the *'ailolo,* and even Kumu Ma'iki, who formalized the *'uniki,* did not participate in it because she was a devout Catholic. The ceremony ends with the *ho'ike* (to show) dances performed in front of hula experts. The *'uniki* is considered a spiritual experience, so the details are generally not publicly shared. In fact, there are kumu who prefer to keep it a secret and are reluctant to explain the ceremonial procedures and its meaning to their students. Today, kumu have simplified or eliminated several of the *'uniki* rituals; the element most likely to be retained is the *ho'ike.*

Once the title *kumu hula* is conferred, the responsibilities of teaching, transmitting, innovating, and so forth need to be assumed. These responsibilities are the subject of this chapter. In Chapter One, the teaching process involving adults as a group was described, but an individual could request private lessons; this could be expensive since the lessons are usually charged hourly. The program that provides continuity and could potentially affect the future and direction of the halau is the work with *keiki* (children). Leiola Hula Halau accepts only *keiki* from three to twelve years old. Teenagers are not accepted because their interest tends to wane and wander at that age level, and there are too many distractions and pressures from peer groups. Since

---

[9] *'Uniki* means "to tie." Presumably knowledge is "tied" to the student through strenuous training.

parents chauffeur their children to the classes, they become indirectly involved in the halau's activities.

However, parents are not allowed to interfere or divert attention from the classroom instruction. Kumu Leiola does not permit parents to be in the room during lesson time; they must wait in the adjoining room or outside. Only on special occasions are they allowed to observe the practices. But parents' assistance is vital in the preparation for outside performances. They provide transportation and other logistical support and help in staging, costume changes, and in the setup of equipment.

There are two distinct types of halau activities involving students. First, there are the practices in the halau, which are basically teaching the dance fundamentals and can be accomplished in a reasonable time frame. Students who want to learn only the fundamentals are short-timers and are there for a few months. They do not have the time or the inclination to make a long-term commitment; they view hula lessons as a recreational activity and do not seek proficiency. Kumu Leiola elaborates on this. "I want to make the distinction between halau and parks and recreation very clear. The halau is where you learn the values like discipline, and you seek to excel, whereas, parks and recreation is for fun, for exercise, and for relief from stress. There is a big difference."

Then, there are other activities: the outside public and private performances and the hula competitions. They provide visibility for the halau and intensive training for the students. Performances are sometimes provided as a free community service as a way of publicizing the halau. For example, in Tucson, there is Tucson Meets Yourself, a multi-ethnic festival held in October, and in Phoenix, there is the Aloha Festival in March. These are community-wide events, attracting thousands of people, but there is a difference in the degree of exposure for the halau. The Tucson festival features many ethnic dance groups, but because there are few Polynesian dance groups, the chances for a hula group to gain attention are much greater. Although the Aloha Festival includes ethnic dance groups, the number of Polynesian dance groups is so large in Phoenix that they dominate the festival, and a Tucson hula group would have a difficult time competing for attention.

Another form of free public performances given by the halau are the dances carried out in hula competitions. The halau are publicized and, at the same time, the students receive additional training while preparing for the contest. However, the majority of performances are paid engagements called "gigs," fulfilling entertainment requests made by companies, organizations, and individuals responsible for organizing personal celebrations. These paid events are held in hotels, restaurants, clubhouses, or recreation centers, places where there is an appropriate dance floor.

To aid in personnel administration, an applicant registering for Leiola Hula Halau has to fill out a standard application form that covers their address, contact information, medical condition, payment arrangement, liability waiver, and confidentiality agreement. For serious-minded applicants, there is a "Performance Group Membership Contract." Those who choose to be members of the performance group are assessed a one-time, nonrefundable membership fee. The fee is used to defray the expenses of providing members with their costumes and adornments or accessories. Kumu Leiola, with occasional help from a seamstress, makes all the costumes and adornments. The materials have to be specially ordered from Hawai'i. If a member quits, is suspended, or is dismissed, the member must return all costumes.

On the instructional side, the requirements for performers are quite detailed and include the mastery of hula steps; rules on level of the eyes, hand style, and motions; proper body alignment; correct foot and toe positions; and how to dance in a line and in formation. Practices are needed to dance as a group because the movements have to be in unison.

In regard to performances, there is a "Guideline for Performers and Performances." Included in this document are the following rules:

- Mandatory attendance at all performances
- Punctuality at all practices
- CD to be used only for practice purposes and not to be shared
- To be quiet and to stay together at performances
- Absolutely no drugs or alcohol
- Members are responsible for bringing and caring for their assigned costumes, accessories, and instruments

There is a separate contract, a "Guidelines of Hawaiian and Polynesian Costumes, Outfits, and Adornment," which further details and reinforces the importance of the care and use of the costumes and adornments. Outfits cannot be altered, and when necessary, they need to be laundered and ironed. Tahitian and Maori costumes are to be purchased by the performer and are their property and must be kept in acceptable condition. In all, the rules are extensive, covering a wide range of topics. The rules make clear behavior is monitored and a high degree of professionalism is expected.

Kumu Leiola insists, "Authenticity is necessary and an important component of all our performances." She believes the history and practices of the past should be honored. *Hula kahiko* is stark, forceful, and simple, accompanied by chanting and accented by drumming on a gourd or drum. The old chants are in Hawaiian and cannot be done in English—it would lose its authenticity and beauty. "The *hula kahiko* is danced and the chanting done without wearing adornments. Jewelry including wedding bands/rings is not allowed and, furthermore, make-up is not allowed, for it was not used in ancient times. To be authentic, certain things are allowed and disallowed in regards to cosmetics and treatment for face, eyes, hair, and nails. No piercings are allowed, and tattoos must be concealed by cosmetics or by the costume. If any of these guidelines or ground rules is violated, the student is not allowed to perform," says Kumu Leiola. To some, these rules seem to be overly concerned with minor details, but to Kumu Leiola, details are important, and authenticity must be maintained.

The guidelines are in a manual, clearly telling the performers what is to be expected, so there will be few surprises. The performers are expected to respect the kumu and their fellow performers and to always exhibit decorum. But how prepared can a student be for such treatment and expectations? When an applicant registers, she or he is given a three months' probation or trial period. If necessary, Kumu Leiola may extend the trial period to adequately evaluate the student's interest and commitment. She always encourages a promising student to be a performer and to join the Performance Group. For those who stay for the long haul, they are recognized as advanced students and are called upon to perform as a select team for events calling for a smaller number of performers.

The preparation and presenting of the performance bring together all the responsibilities of the kumu, including teaching, research, selecting the music and dances, choreographing, preparing the accompanying instruments, handling the costumes and accessories, the audio equipment, and other innumerable logistical matters. In addition, there are the administrative details to be managed—rental agreement, bill payments, and other contractual agreements.

The most time-consuming responsibilities are teaching and research, the keys to a successful performance. Once the dances and music have been selected, the instructional phase begins. All kumu agree language is critical—the words, ancient stories, and poetry of the *mele* and chants have to be translated into English and explained. Kuma Leiola spends considerable time in language research. Many Hawaiian words have several meanings; which meaning to use depends on the context. Therefore, familiarity with the language and an understanding of the culture are essential. She translates Hawaiian words into English and writes them on the blackboard or on sheets of paper to be reproduced. This is done for all the songs used in the dances. The background of the stories is explained and in the process, various aspects of Hawaiian culture and the environment are discussed. All the materials are reviewed at the end of the preparatory session.

At a minimum, students should know basic Hawaiian words relating to the dances and music, and even understand the *kaona* (hidden meaning) in the *mele,* of which there are many, making it all the more challenging. A simple word like *rain* is complex. It could mean light rain, which connotes joy or life, or it could be heavy rain, which connotes grief, sorrow, and darkness. Moreover, many rains are associated with a specific island or location. Hence, native elements have to be explained, and the students often have to use visualization to get a feel for the word. Then the dancer uses eyes and facial expressions along with his or her hands, feet, and body movements to paint a picture of the object or emotion involved in the story being portrayed. This is why Hawaiian words have to be accurately translated and explained.

It is difficult for the non-natives to capture and inwardly experience the sights and sounds of the islands, the whole environment, as well as the feelings or emotions of the natives. The dance students in Tucson, Arizona, do not know what it feels like to walk on the sandy beach, to see and hear the waves coming in, and to feel the gentle ocean breeze. Kumu Leiola has to instruct the students to lower their arms from head level to waist level when depicting waves. It is, after all, not a tidal wave! The songs tell of the fragrance of *maile*—but how is the student in a desert environment going to know the fragrance of *maile* leaves? How do you describe the smell of a *pikake,* a jasmine flower used in leis? Computer technology can help students to visually relate to the sceneries and flora depicted in the chants, songs, and dances, but it cannot replicate actually experiencing the elements in Hawai'i. Furthermore, the expressive dance movements are best taught personally and not by watching the screen.

The mindset of the dancer is crucial. It gives expression to the movements; vibrant energy has to flow, and the dancer not only has to be mindful of the movements but also has to focus on the present moment. The dancer cannot be thinking about what he or she will be doing tomorrow; the moment is now! This mental discipline is just as important as the mastery of specific steps and motions. The kumu has to instill this mindset. The emotional component has to go with the intellectual knowledge base.

The kumu serves as the motivator. Within their interest, every student should strive to achieve their stated goal. "One needs to know before they dance why they are dancing," says Kumu Leiola. "It concerns me when people don't know what they want. Students should derive a sense of accomplishment." There should be a larger purpose than simply learning the dance movements for one's own pleasure. They should feel a connection with the Hawaiian heritage, while simultaneously finding satisfaction in helping the audience to appreciate Hawaiian culture. These larger reasons are what keep students dancing year after year.

Another task of the kumu is that of a disciplinarian. The practice of maintaining discipline and attention by using the split-bamboo stick to strike the dancers' arms, legs, or other body parts had ceased long ago. Even though the halau is run as a tight ship, with stringent rules and discipline, each student is valued as a member of the *'ohana nui* (extended family). The kumu has to be firm and establish standards to adhere to and to maintain, for once discipline is lost, it's difficult to recover. But at the same time, the kumu has to be kind and compassionate; there is a fine line and a balancing act.

Furthermore, the kumu is a counselor, not getting involved in personal matters but willing to listen when needed. When a member seems troubled, Kumu Leiola takes the person aside and listens to the concerns. Personal problems do affect the mindset, so they should not be ignored. Personal relationship involves respect for one another, and respect for others is part of being an *'ohana* member. The Hawaiian way of showing respect is by using the familial form of address. Seniors are referred to as "auntie" and "uncle." The kumu becomes "Auntie Leiola," although Kumu Leiola says, "I don't appreciate being called 'auntie' by the *haumana* because such familiarity doesn't evoke respect." Once a relationship is established, it is acceptable to use "auntie." Regardless of the form of address, the sheer energy required to prepare for performances and competition makes for a sense of familial unity. There is an awareness of being together and, most important, a sense of belonging. What each kumu desires is a tight-knit group, whose members respect and support each other.

In regards to the concept of *'ohana,* an interesting comparison can be made between kumu and its *'ohana* and the Japanese *sensei* (teacher) and its traditional *odori* (dance) family. *Sensei* is a revered figure, and in Japanese interpersonal relationships, the hierarchical structure is formal; there is no "auntie" or "uncle."

Japanese would not use familial and informal form of address with seniors and authoritative figures. Such familiar form of address is thought to be rude and considered bad manners. Japanese recognize status level by specific honorific forms of address, which are used between senior and junior, or between superior and subordinate. The founder or current head of a traditional Japanese dance school is referred to as *iemoto* (grand master). The *iemoto* passes on the tradition and style of the school to the disciples, and a few become *sensei* and are blessed and recognized by the *iemoto*. The *sensei* can then recognize and designate their own accredited teachers, who in turn can become teachers with their own followers. This teacher–disciple relationship is somewhat similar to that of the kumu–advanced student relationship.

In Tucson, there is only one traditional Japanese *odori* group, the Suzuyuki-kai (Suzuyuki Association). Mari Kaneta, the founder of Suzuyuki-kai, was bestowed the ceremonial name, "Suzuyuki," by her *iemoto*. The *iemoto* genealogical line extends four centuries in Japan and covers all of Japan. The line is so broad that occasionally, there have been problems determining the successor *iemoto*. Mari Kaneta (Suzuyuki) learned the dance styles from her *iemoto* and then developed her own styles and passed them to her students, which is similar to the process followed by kumu. The recognition ceremony of the Japanese *odori* group, where certificates of achievement are presented, ceremonial names bestowed, and dances performed by the honorees is somewhat similar to the ritualistic ʻuniki graduation ceremony of the kumu.[10]

Therefore, there are striking similarities and some differences between the Hawaiian and Japanese dance groups. Both the kumu and *sensei* receive their training from their master teacher,

---

[10] Interview with Mari Kaneta, June 13, 2018.

help preserve their respective culture and tradition, develop their own styles, and transmit all of these to their students. The biggest difference is in interpersonal relationships. Both are hierarchical relationships, but the relationship between kumu and *haumana* in the halau is informal and familial, whereas the relationship between *sensei* and *seito* (student) in the Japanese dance group is formal and structural.

In summary, the kumu determines the direction of the halau and is the "glue" that holds the organization together. The *kuleana* (responsibilities) are many, onerous, and demanding. Professor Amy K. Stillman made a list of responsibilities of the kumu in the form of questions and came up with 127 questions! Included in the list were responsibilities to the following: the kumu hula, the *haumana,* the *mele* and hula, the community, the sources (stories, memories, and histories), all items used in hula, and the Hawaiian language and tradition.[11] There are critics who say the title of kumu hula has been debased by those not qualified and by those who have not taken the responsibilities seriously. With the proliferation of kumu hula, serious discussions about standards have ensued. The critics say the new kumu hula are not undergoing rigorous training over an extended period; they lack the long apprenticeship of the old days. Moreover, in gravitating toward showmanship, they are neglecting their responsibilities toward traditional hula and its customs. However, there remains a strong core of hula teachers who have assumed their responsibilities and have been closely tied to the traditional customs and styles, while embracing innovations.

---

[11] Amy Ku'uleialoha Stillman, "On the Kuleana of a Kumu Hula." https://amykstillman.wordpress.com (2011).

CHAPTER THREE

DEVELOPMENT OF HULA

Hula is the language of the heart and therefore the heartbeat of the Hawaiian people.(King David Kalakaua)

Where hula originated is problematic—some say it came from Moloka'i, others Kaua'i, and some mention places outside of Polynesia—but most experts agree it is indigenously Hawaiian. How it began is shrouded in ancient myths and legends. According to one account, the dance originated when the goddess Hi'iaka danced to calm her fiery older sister, Pele, the goddess of the volcano. This story is told in many *mele* and chants. In the pantheon of Hawaiian gods and goddesses, Laka is another goddess with a prominent place in several chants and dances. She is the goddess of love, forests, and plants, and is considered to be the goddess of hula. In order to recount these myths and legends, the natives founded the hula dance form.

Prior to the arrival of Westerners, the Hawaiians had no written language. Therefore, there are no extant records or documents. The ancient Hawaiians had to memorize stories, rituals, genealogy, and histories and pass them on orally. They did this surprisingly well, but information was still lost. The dance became a means of communication between the deities and worshipers, principally the *kahuna* (priest), and began to be used frequently for religious purposes. This practice of using dance in religious ceremonies as a means of communication between gods and priests is found in many other early societies and is, therefore, not unique to the Hawaiians. Hula was performed for the gods and goddesses and not for the people; it was a temple dance and was not performed publicly.

The word *hula* itself is Hawaiian. It was not in general use until the mid-1800s. The word used for dance previously was *ha'a* that was used to describe the dancing with bent knees.[12] The ancient dance was, indeed, characterized by a posture or stance of bent knees. The dance was accompanied by chanting and drumming with gourd and was called *hula 'olapa* and later, probably in the mid-nineteenth century, came to be referred to as *hula kahiko*. The various types of chanting and drumming have a mesmerizing effect, and even today its beauty is recognized. The drumming is done with unique percussion instruments, including the *pahu* (drum), *ipu* (gourd), and *ipu heke* (double gourd). Kumu Leiola often begins her program by paying homage to the ancient dance—she chants and beats on the *ipu* while sitting. *Hula noho* (sitting hula) was a common way of performing hula in the early days.

Hula kahiko is the ancient hula, but the degree of its authenticity has become a subject of controversy. There are those who want to go back to the "original" *hula kahiko* and to maintain its pure form. They view any changes to the ancient form to be an abomination. But even in the earliest days of *kahiko,* changes, however little, must have occurred and were never recorded. Dance forms, after all, evolve over a period of time. The best to

---

[12] Mary Kawena Pukui and Samuel H. Elbert, *Hawaiian Dictionary,* rev. ed. (Honolulu: University of Hawaii Press, 1986), 44.

be hoped for is to go back to the forms and styles first recorded and make them the benchmark. Adherents of *hula kahiko* today would say they do *'ai kahiko* (in the ancient style). There is a need, even a necessity, for innovation to take place if *hula kahiko* is to be performed publicly and not become a relic. More footsteps were included for advanced students. A supporter of *hula kahiko,* Kumu Leiola says, "I do *kahiko* in the ancient style, thus maintaining its authenticity." But what does doing *kahiko* in the ancient style mean? It has become a ubiquitous phrase, but the protocols are not clearly defined, so the controversy as to what is proper and correct continues.

It is not true that only men were allowed to do the hula in early times. Although, at the beginning, only men were allowed to perform during *heiau* (temple) worship and to do the chanting, there are evidences of women dancing as early as the late eighteenth century. By the time foreigners came to Hawai'i, hula was being performed outside the temple, and women were involved. By then, it was for the public. The *ali'i* (ruling elites) supported the hula, but the *maka'ainana* (commoners) themselves became passionate about it.[13] Captain James Cook, during his expedition to Kaua'i in 1778, noted in his journal that women were seen dancing. Louis Choris, a French artist, did drawings in 1816 depicting female dancers, some with tattoos. When the missionaries arrived in 1820 from distant New England, they also found women dancing.

Missionaries were appalled by the hula dancing. In their journals, they described the women dancers wearing short skirts wrapped around the waist and extending to the knees. The skirts were called *pa'u* and were made of *kapa* (tapa bark). Shockingly, the women dancers were topless. The men were clad only in tapa *malo* (loincloths). All the dancers wore leis, which

---

[13] Emerson, *Unwritten*, 26.

are wreaths for the head and for the neck, and they wore necklaces, bracelets, and anklets made of dog's teeth, whale's teeth, shell, or bone.[14] It is interesting to note that even today, these adornments are used, except the dog's teeth has been replaced by shells or plastic replicas of dog's teeth. The missionaries considered hula to be indecent, lewd, and "lascivious," a term used by Rev. Hiram Bingham. They believed hula promoted pagan worship and found it closely associated with ancient Hawaiian gods and goddesses and, consequently, a heathen dance. Rev. Bingham wrote: "The whole arrangement and process of their old hulas were designed to promote lasciviousness, and of course the practice of them could not flourish in modest communities. They (hula) had been interwoven too with their superstitions, and made subservient to the honor of their gods, and then rulers, either living or departed or deified."[15] Hula was lascivious because it promoted physical enjoyment.

The immediate reaction of the missionaries was to cover the women dancers. Early photographs showed how fully covered the dancers were. They wore Mother Hubbard gowns, or if they wore skirts, it was of taffeta, which gave a stiff appearance, and leggings were used to cover the legs. The transformation was quite drastic.

But there were missionaries who found redeeming qualities in hula. Rev. Charles Samuel Stewart described hula as follows: "The motions of the dance were slow and graceful, and, in this instance, free from indelicacy of action; and the song, or rather recitative, accompanied by much gesticulation, was dignified and harmonious in its number."[16] The second generation

---

[14] Emerson, 40–41.

[15] Peter T. Young, "Hula—How the Missionaries Felt." imagesofoldhawaii.com/hula-pahu (December 8, 2013).

[16] Young (2013).

of missionary families was even more sympathetic and appreciative of hula. Nathaniel B. Emerson, the son of missionary parents, wrote: "The hula was a religious service, in which poetry, music, pantomime, and the dance lent themselves, under the forms of dramatic arts to the refreshment of men's minds."[17] The research by Emerson, ironically, helped to preserve the ancient chants and *mele*. His work, in describing in detail the halau and the different types of hula, remains a valuable source on ancient hula.

Although the missionaries condemned hula, they did not have the authority to ban it. However, they did succeed in getting hula banned by converting a few powerful *ali'i* (chiefs) to Christianity. The event that opened the way for the conversion of the *ali'i* was the abolishment of the *kapu* (sacred or holy) system. There is a misconception that the missionaries undermined and caused the collapse of the *kapu* system. The *kapu* system was a comprehensive set of rules governing almost all aspects of life, and included moral, ethical, civil, ceremonial, and dietary rules, many with religious implications. It consisted of hundreds of rules telling people what they can do and cannot do. The commoners wanted relief from this oppressive and burdensome system.

With the death of Kamehameha the Great, the founder of the dynasty, his son Liholiho ascended the throne and took the reign name of Kamehameha II. Kamehameha II decided this was the best time to abolish the *kapu* tradition, and he did it with one simple act, by sitting and eating publicly with Ka'ahumanu, the queen regent at a lu'au.[18] It violated the taboo forbidding

---

[17] Emerson, *Unwritten*, 11–12.

[18] Queen regent could be called *kuhina nui* (prime minister). See Pukui, *Hawaiian Dictionary,* 173. Ka'ahumanu was Kamehameha II's stepmother. She created this position, making her co-equal with the king.

men and women eating together in public, an act punishable by death. Of course, the king could not be put to death, and the gods did not retaliate, so the taboo was officially broken, and the *kapu* system overturned. Kamehameha II had the support of Ka'ahumanu, his mother Keopuolani, and the high priest Hewahewa, but Ka'ahumanu, who had become a Christian, was the prime mover; she led the movement to end the *kapu* system.

This happened in 1819, a year before the missionaries arrived. Therefore, the *kapu* system basically collapsed within itself once the process was started. Ka'ahumanu ordered all the *heiau* (temples) and idols destroyed. The Hawaiians were shocked and disoriented by this social and cultural upheaval, and a spiritual vacuum was created. An opportune moment was created, and the missionaries quickly filled this religious void, especially making inroads with the *ali'i*. Since hula was closely associated with the religious practices of the *heiau* and was already condemned by the missionaries, it was easily suppressed. As a result, hula largely disappeared from the public scene.

But hula did not die out. Instead, it was taught and practiced in secret and was performed at parties given by the upper class. At various times, attempts were made to ban or regulate the performance of hula. A law was enacted in 1859, banning the public performance of hula, and later a law was passed requiring a license. Another regulation required a fee to be paid for each performance. All these efforts did not stop the teaching and practice of hula, and the hula tradition continued to be passed on furtively.

Hula began to be performed publicly during the reign of King David Kalakaua (1874–91). He moved to restore Hawaiian cultural tradition and was patron of the arts, and in this capacity, he helped to revive hula. King Kalakaua, had an outgoing personality and was curious enough to try new things, and it was not surprising he took a fancy for hula. He was musically inclined and played some instruments. His coronation in 1883 featured three days of hula, a total of 262 performances, and of these, some thirty were a new hula called *hula ku'i* (joined hula), which mixed together old and new hula steps and was accompanied by guitar, ukulele, *ipu,* and *pahu*.[19] Furthermore, another dance was introduced, the *hula nema nema*.[20] The jubilee celebration in 1886 had as its special attraction both ancient chants and new forms of hula. King Kalakaua was noted for his travels and for holding elaborate lu'aus and grand balls; he loved entertainment. Merrie Monarch was his nickname, and this name is used today for the annual hula competition held on the Big Island—the world's biggest hula competition. Overall, hula enjoyed a vibrant renewal with other parts of the Hawaiian culture, and this period has been rightly called a "renaissance." His sister Queen Lili'uokalani was his successor, and she continued to support the arts and brought together the dance forms of ancient Hawai'i with that of the West. Actually, she was more talented musically than Kalakaua.

The genealogy of hula masters can be traced back to the dancers of the Kalakaua and Lili'uokalani courts. With the end of the monarchy, Julie Keahi Luahine is said to be the last court dancer. Present-day kumu hula can trace their genealogical line back to Keahi Luahine. Keahi taught 'Iolani Lauhine and Mary Kawena Pukui. They in turn taught and influenced Edith Kanaka'ole, Lokalia Montgomery, Nona Beamer, George Na'ope, Ma'iki Aiu Lake, and George Holokai, all of whom became eminent kumu hula. Most of the contemporary kumu hula emanated from these master teachers. It is quite remarkable to see clearly how the hula tradition was passed from one generation to another. One of the principle responsibilities of a kumu hula

---

[19] Emerson, *Unwritten,* 250–51.

[20] Pukui, *Hawaiian Dictionary,* 88,174.

is to pass on the knowledge and skills to other kumu. As seen, this has been done successfully.

The end of the monarchical period at the turn of the twentieth century witnessed the gradual decline of many aspects of traditional Hawaiian culture, and much of it fell into disfavor. After the brief flourishing of Hawaiian culture during the Kalakaua reign, the enormous impact of the West changed the native culture and arts. The traditional hula movements were maintained, but from the time of Kalakaua, they became mixed with Western dance steps. The Hawaiians were introduced to melody and the pentatonic scale, a far cry from the two-and-three-note scales of the chants. Many of the changes in music resulted from the influence of Christian hymns. With changes in the music, a new dance form emerged, the *hula 'auana* (modern hula)—the word *'auana* means "to wander" or "drift."[21] In the eyes of the traditionalist, this modern hula did, indeed, "wander" from the ancient style.

During the reign of King Kalakaua, new musical instruments were introduced. The ukulele, a four strings instrument closely resembling a small guitar, probably came from Portugal. In Hawaiian, it meant "jumping flea," presumably referring to the rapid movement of the fingers over the strings. Another stringed instrument introduced was the guitar. Its origin is problematic. The traditional style of playing the guitar was later changed when Hawaiian musicians loosened their strings and began to improvise with open tunings. This style of playing became known as *kiho'alu* (slack key) and was kept private and was not played in public until the 1950s. It has become a uniquely Hawaiian musical sound.

In addition, another part of the Hawaiian instrumental sound is the steel guitar, a favorite of Kalakaua. Its origin is unknown,

---

[21] Pukui, 30.

but its sound is identified with country music. To summarize, at the turn of the century, the use of stringed instruments, namely the ukulele and guitar, became dominant and replaced the percussion instruments used in *kahiko.* The ancient Hawaiian chants almost disappeared, and the *mele* changed as Hawaiian words were used less frequently. Attention to *kahiko* faded while interest in new forms of hula emerged.

Unfortunately, many of the new songs and hula had little resemblance to traditional Hawaiian music and dance. So-called Hawaiian music and dance swept across America. Hawaiian musicians and dancers went along with the craze—it was, after all, what the public demanded. Commercialization of Hawaiian culture became rampant, and tourism grew. Tourists wanted glamorous and fast-tempo and fast-stepped hula. Showmanship became more important than the conveying of the story or the meaning of the lyrics.

The modern Hawaiian songs called *hapa haole* (half foreign, half Hawaiian) became popular from around the 1920s and held on to its popularity until the 1960s. These songs were sung in Hawaiian or in English. The dance became known as *hapa haole hula,* a hula danced to Hawaiian-type songs but with English lyrics. Even traditional Hawaiian songs were now heard with popular jazz rhythms. They had Hawaiian subject matter, but the words were all in English. This was the Hawaiian music heard around the world on the popular radio program *Hawaii Calls,* which began in 1935, usually broadcasting from the banyan tree at the Moana Hotel in Waikiki. Songs exemplifying the "haole-fication" of the hula were Johnny Noble's "Little Grass Shack in Kealakekua, Hawaii" and R. Alex Anderson's "Lovely Hula Hands," and "The Cockeyed Mayor of Kaunakakai."[22]

---

[22] Jerry Hopkins, *The Hula* (Hong Kong: Apa Productions, 1982), 85–86.

With the tourism industry booming, visitors were welcomed to the islands by hula dancers. When the Matson Navigation passenger liners, Matsonia and Lurline, arrived in Honolulu Harbor in the 1930s and in the early post-World War II years, the tourists were greeted by hula dancers at the dockside. Called "Boat Day," the scene is vividly remembered by Kumu Leiola. She recalled, as a youngster, dancing at the dockside while the Royal Hawaiian Band played and boys dove into the water retrieving coins tossed by the tourists. It was a colorful scene, but for Leiola, it was pure entertainment and a fun time and not a learning experience.

Hula shows flourished nightly at the Waikiki hotels. There was even a daytime hula show, the Kodak Hula Show held in Kapiolani Park, next to Waikiki. It turned out to be the largest hula show of its time, and at its height, attracted at least three thousand spectators weekly. Founded in 1937 by Fritz Herman, vice-president and manager of Kodak Hawaii, it entertained tourists for sixty-five years! The director for more than forty years was Louise Akeo Silva. She got several halau to participate in the shows. The typical show had about twenty dancers, accompanied by a dozen musicians; there were even a couple of chanters. Although the show was mostly *hapa haole hula* and *'auana* dances, it did include *kahiko* dances. The show ended with the dancers holding big Kodak and Hawai'i signs as tourists frantically took pictures. As it turned out, for many tourists, this was their only exposure to hula. But despite the commercialism, the hula dances were authentic—traditional hula mixed with modern Hawaiian hula danced by performers from the halau.

Then it happened—Hollywood discovered Hawai'i. Hula was featured in several movies, with dancers wearing sarongs and grass-skirts (usually made of cellophane), swaying their hips and graceful limbs across the silver screen. The first film glamorizing the hula was Clara Bow in *Hula* (1927) and was followed by several others, such as: Dolores Del Rio in *Bird of Paradise* (1932),

Bing Crosby in *Waikiki Wedding (1937),* and Betty Grable in *Song of the Islands* (1942) that also featured Hilo Hattie.[23] The hula presented in these movies was just for entertainment and said little about Hawaiian culture. The stereotype images of dancers wearing coconut bras and grass-skirts were spread all over the United States and worldwide, and colored the views of two generations. There were posters showing a girl in grass-skirt, wearing a lei, and holding a ukulele with a coconut tree in the background. This was a popular image and was widely distributed. The romanticized image of the 1920s and 1930s was temporarily halted by the outbreak of World War II. Such a fixed view of hula even affected some local Asian families. Parents warned their daughters not to take hula lessons because of its seductive nature. Unfortunately, the stereotypes and assumptions still persist. This glamorous view of hula made the revival of traditional hula all the more difficult.

A move to correct the Hollywood image of hula began in the late 1940s with Aloha Week, a celebration held in Honolulu in October. Initiated by the business community, it brought back traditional Hawaiian culture, and at the same time, it provided an attraction for the tourist industry. Hula played an important part, with hula pageants attracting large crowds. With the generous support of the kumu, several halau participated and over the years, thousands of hula students were involved.[24]

Just when it was looking good for hula, another blow was struck. Rock and roll music arrived in mid-1950s. Hawaiian music literally disappeared. Radio stations no longer played Hawaiian music; it was no longer "cool." The ukulele was replaced by the electric guitar. Enrollment in hula classes declined and purchase of hula instruments dropped significantly. The Elvis Presley

---

[23] Hilo Hattie was noted for her comic hula.

[24] Hopkins, *The Hula,* 99–100.

movie, *Blue Hawai'i* appeared in 1961, and the shock wave continued as the Beatles and other rock musicians became popular. But the biggest damage was the loss of a generation. Many of the young people in Hawai'i lost all interest in Hawaiian music and dance.[25] To recoup from this loss would take time, and it was a struggle to fill the void created by rock and roll music, and to interest the younger generation to listen once again to Hawaiian music.

A major part of the commercialization of hula was the teaching of hula to tourists. Hotels offered hula "classes" to its guests. For the Waikiki hula studios, providing instructors for the classes became quite profitable. At the University of Hawai'i summer session, the gym was filled to capacity with mainland coeds taking classes on hula. The dances, in all instances, were the simpler *hapa haole hula* and included popular numbers like "Hukilau" and "Lovely Hula Hands."

There were a few kumu who, during the early postwar period, continued to teach the traditional hula and the chants. They were 'Iolani Luahine, Tom Hiona, Henry Pa, Edith Kanaka'ole, and George Holokai, among others. Ma'iki Aiu Lake taught *hula ku'i,* mixing the traditional with the modern. It was not the popular thing to do, but these pioneers realized the importance of being linked to the past. Once the past is lost, it may never be recovered.

Kent Ghirard, a haole kumu and his Hula Nani Halau performed at the hotels and worked with the Hawai'i Visitors Bureau, greeting tourists. Ghirard was good at producing shows, and his troupe was probably the best-known group at that time. He was criticized for focusing on performance rather than on interpretation of the words of the *mele*. This is a common criticism of those who were creative and added to *hula kahiko*. Nevertheless,

---

[25] Hopkins, 124.

he did teach the old-style hula.[26] So *hula kahiko* was taught but sometimes in modified, subdued form.

It is not clear when it started, but Tahitian and Maori (natives of New Zealand) dance began to have influence on hula. These Polynesian dances began to be popular in the 1960s. Students requested lesson in Tahitian and Maori dances, hence the halau began to offer them. First, Tahitian and then Maori dances became a part of the repertoire. Audiences found the dances exotic and exciting, especially the hip movements and costume in Tahitian and the poi ball of the Maori. In some programs, these dances began to have a prominent role and were presented as the finale.

These Polynesian dances are not part of Hawaiian culture. If the dance program is billed as "Hula Performances" or "Hawaiian Dances," Tahitian and Maori dances should not have a major role, surely not as a finale. A general term like Polynesian is proper for a program that equally represents dances of Hawai'i, Tahiti, Samoa, and other Pacific Islands—they are all Polynesian. Leiola Hula Halau offers Tahitian and Maori dance lessons when requested by students, but they are offered as a supplement and are never considered a major part of the program.

To sum up: today, hula has become probably the best-known segment of Hawaiian culture. Hula began as a ceremonial dance closely associated with temple worship, and by the time Westerners arrived in Hawai'i, men and women were performing the hula outside the temple. In the ensuing 150 years, from the coming of the missionaries in 1820 to the revival of the hula in the 1970s, the traditional *hula kahiko* experienced a steady decline in public participation and interest. There was a renewal of interest during the Kalakaua reign of the late 1880s, but at that time, the suppression of traditional hula by

---

[26] Hopkins, 99–100.

the missionaries and local elites was replaced by the influence of Western music. It was not suppression but the infusion of another mode of dancing and music.

Up to this point, traditional hula continued to be taught and practiced albeit being done privately and secretly. Transmission of knowledge continued, but there was practically no innovation in traditional hula. The introduction of Western music and instruments, however, resulted in new forms of dances that distinctly departed from traditional *kahiko*. In place of chants, melodious tunes were sung. Furthermore, hand, foot, and body movements became fluid and smoother. *Hapa haole hula* and *'auana* became dominant, and innovations in these dances flourished, sometimes going to the extreme of being glamorized and made into a vaudeville act. The gap between traditional *kahiko* and modern *'auana* became larger. But how do these changes help hula to reflect and express Hawaiian culture and history? How "Hawaiian" is present-day hula? These were questions asked after a century and a half of development.

CHAPTER FOUR

HAWAIIAN RENAISSANCE AND HULA

> I am, in depth, a product of Hawaii—an American, yes, who is a citizen of the fiftieth State, but I am also a Hawaiian, somewhat by blood, and in large measure by sentiment. Of this, I am proud.
> John Dominis Holt IV (1964)

After Hawai'i achieved statehood in 1959, the demographics of the population changed significantly. Caucasians became the largest racial group as mainlanders moved to Hawai'i. At the same time, tourism accelerated with more visitors arriving. The influx of tourists and those who decided to move to Hawai'i did not help to promote interest in Hawaiian culture. Instead, these developments led to an increasing disinterest in Hawaiian arts and tradition and to an emphasis on Americanization. According to hula advocates, this period from the end of World War II to the advent of statehood was the low point for traditional hula. But the decline of hula started earlier as discussed in Chapter Three. Public performances were banned in the mid-nineteenth century, and from time to time, other restrictions were put in place to discourage hula dancing. Hula was looked upon with disfavor by segments of the population. Some hula supporters thought hula would surely disappear.

In the meantime, a similar experience overtook the Hawaiian language. Interest in the Hawaiian language declined, and its use was discouraged. There is a mistaken impression that the missionaries forced the natives to give up their language in favor of English. The missionaries actually preached in Hawaiian, and by printing the Bible in Hawaiian, they promoted the reading of the Hawaiian language. By the late nineteenth century, the literacy rate had increased, and it was surprisingly high. It was the American businessmen who pushed for banning the Hawaiian language. The Americans wanted to instill their values, to Americanize the natives, and there was no better way to do this then to make English the only official language.

After the kingdom was overthrown in 1893 and annexed in 1898, English was made the official language and was mandated in the public schools. The Hawaiian language, although not officially banned from school and government, could only be used in exceptional situations and had to have official approval. One would expect, at the least, Hawaiian to be taught at Kamehameha School in Honolulu, a school open only to pupils of Hawaiian or part-Hawaiian ancestry, but it was not taught there. Officials at the school went overboard and placed restrictions on other facets of Hawaiian culture, for example, forbidding stand-up hula. Only sitting down hula could be performed. In schools all over the community, discipline and punishment awaited those who used Hawaiian. The number of native speakers of Hawaiian dropped to less than one-tenth of one percent of the total population. Several in the community considered Hawaiian to be a rapidly dying language.

But the situation changed dramatically in the 1970s with revival of interest and an enthusiasm for traditional Hawaiian culture as Native Hawaiians rediscovered their heritage. In 1978, Hawaiian was made the official state language with English. Historians have called this revival the "Second Hawaiian Renaissance." The "First Hawaiian Renaissance" took place during the reign of King Kalakaua when there was a renewal of interest in hula and other traditional aspects of Hawaiian culture. Unfortunately, it lasted only a short time and came to an end with the passing of the monarchy.

Although this chapter is primarily concerned with the renewed interest in traditional hula, it must be understood in the context of the broad changes taking place in several areas of Hawaiian culture. There was renewed interest in the Hawaiian language with soaring enrollment in Hawaiian language courses at the university. It could barely keep up with demands, and the instructional staff grew from one to more than a dozen. Interest in Hawaiian music with Hawaiian lyrics and chants and accompanied by slack key and steel guitars grew quickly and recordings of hula songs and chants accelerated. Traditional crafts expanded, for example, Guitar and Lute Workshop, a local company, made guitars and restored old instruments. Interest in canoeing revived, and there was great interest in the voyaging of *Hokule'a*, a replica of a large, ancient Polynesian canoe. *Hokule'a* completed a round trip to Tahiti, demonstrating the remarkable navigational skills of the Polynesians; it was, indeed, an accomplishment to be proud of.

As to why these changes took place, the events of that time have to be examined. There were several movements at work, most of them developed in the 1960s. First, there was the civil rights movement with African Americans demanding equality and justice. Second, ethnic groups, such as Japanese Americans, Chicanos, and Puerto Ricans, were expressing their grievances and demanding their rights, for example, Japanese Americans seeking redress and justice for the internment experience during

World War II. Third, the rise of ethnic studies in colleges and universities, and the younger generation becoming interested in their heritage and "roots." Fourth, the Vietnam War resulted in the use of demonstrations to protest and to question authority. Finally, Native Hawaiians resorted to political activism to assert their land and sovereignty rights and to gain greater autonomy.

All of these movements created a milieu where Hawaiians, like other ethnic groups, became conscious of their racial identity and became proud of it. They now had pride in their culture and in their heritage. "On Being Hawaiian," an essay written in 1964 by John Dominis Holt IV, stirred this self-identity and pride. He was a *hapa haole* (mixed Native Hawaiian) and the author of novels and books on Hawaiian history and culture. His essay set the tone for the Hawaiian Renaissance; his contribution was seminal, and he was later honored as a "living treasure" by the state of Hawai'i.

An interesting aspect of the renewed interest was the establishment of *kane hula* (men's hula) in the world of hula. For a long period, it was considered sissy for men to participate in hula, although men were once active dancers during the early days of temple worship. Hula dancing came to be thought of as a feminine dance meant only for women. A small group of men, Darrell Lupenui, John Ka'imikaua, Thaddeus Wilson, and O'Brian Eselu, formed the Men of Waimapuna (Spring Water) to perform men's hula. It disbanded after a year, and the leaders went their separate ways. Meanwhile, Robert Cazimero and John Topolinski worked to make men's hula respectable.[27]

Soon, in 1976, Merrie Monarch Festival was opened for men to compete. At that time, Kumu Cazimero had the only all-male

---

[27] Kumu hula Robert Cazimero and his brother Roland formed the famous musical duo, the Brothers Cazimero. Kumu hula John Topolinski was a high school teacher of Hawaiian history and culture and an expert on *lei hulu* (feather lei).

halau, the Halau Na Kamalei o Lililehua.[28] They were the winners in the *hula 'auana* competition in their initial entry in the Merrie Monarch Festival. They grew rapidly during the renaissance but declined after the 1970s. For men's groups, it remains a challenge to this day to attract and retain men; other concerns, mainly jobs and sports, do constantly intervene.

Nevertheless, the interest developed in the 1970s has left a legacy. The Men of Waimapuna was reconstituted under Kumu Darrell Lupenui and has expanded beyond windward O'ahu and has established halau on the mainland and overseas. It won the top honor in the 1986 Merrie Monarch Festival under the leadership of Lupenui. His successors have led the Men of Waimapuna to other awards, winning the top honor in Merrie Monarch several times. Meanwhile, the other members of the original Men of Waimapuna, Wilson and Eselu, formed their own group called Na Wai 'Eha 'O Puna (The Four Waters of Puna). Men's hula brings a powerful dance style with athleticism and depicts old warrior skills. It has been characterized as bombastic, but it can show softness and gracefulness in love stories. As for the future, a new generation of male kumu has emerged, and this bode well for *kane hula*.

What was surprising in the Hawaiian Renaissance was the interest shown in *hula kahiko*. It at least matched the interest shown in modern and *hapa haole hula*. Enthusiasts wanted to master the ancient dance movements, to learn to chant, and to play the percussion instruments. There were those who advocated going back to the "original" *kahiko*, but as previously discussed, this is impossible. There are innovations with each generation, and the *kahiko* of today cannot be the same as those of the late eighteenth century. Change is inevitable, and all that

---

[28] Kumu Tom Hiona had a male troupe in the 1930s. See Hopkins, *The Hula*, 94.

can be hoped for is to be as authentic as possible and to maintain cultural integrity.

For the first time, official recognition began to be given to hula luminaries by the state of Hawai'i. In 1970, 'Iolani Luahine and Lokalia Montgomery were the first to receive the highest honors and were followed by others, including Edith Kanaka'ole, Mai'ike Aiu Lake, who was called the "mother of the Hawaiian Renaissance," and Mary Kawena Pukui. The state government began the designation of "Living Treasure of Hawai'i" and the first designee was 'Iolani Luahine. Organizations were formed to promote, maintain, and perpetuate the hula. In 1968, the State Council on Hawaiian Heritage was created. It was a loosely organized group of cultural leaders whose task was to raise funds and to distribute grants to workshops expanding the teaching of hula. The focus was on going back to the basic functions of a kumu—to have the best-qualified and talented kumu teach dancers the traditional hula and train them to be teachers.

Nonprofit organizations advancing Hawaiian music and dance began appearing. The Hawaiian Music Foundation founded in 1971 offered classes in the making and playing of ancient instruments and classes in *hula kahiko.* The Kalihi-Palama Cultural and Arts Society, a neighborhood group, in 1976, started a series of kumu–led workshops and sponsored hula contests. It recognized the accomplishments of hula leaders in two large volumes, which had excellent portrait photographs by Shuzo Uemoto with seventy-seven kumu interviews in Volume I and fifty-seven interviews in Volume II. These short biographical sketches and comments provide valuable historical resources on the leadership of the hula community of the 1980s and 1990s.[29]

---

[29] Jan M. Itagaki and Lovina Lependu, eds. *Nana I Na Loea Hula* (Look to the Hula Resources). vol. I (Honolulu: Edward Enterprises, 1984). vol. II (Honolulu: Everbest Printing Co., 1997).

The contribution of Ma'iki Aiu Lake in establishing the protocols and vigorously training large classes of potential kumu has been previously discussed. She used unorthodox approaches, like blackboards and printed materials, and required note taking. She advertised in local newspapers to attract potential kumu and was criticized initially, but it worked! Others followed, including Kumu Kau'i Zuttermeister who advertised in local papers for students; in the late 1970s, she had classes with about 150 students. Hula masters began to use innovative methods and began to think outside the box.

MERRIE MONARCH FESTIVAL

An event was needed to bring together the hula community, a gathering that went beyond the individual hula recitals. The annual Merrie Monarch Festival, held in Hilo on the Big Island, met this need. It was co-founded in 1964 by George Na'ope and Dorothy Thompson. Na'ope and Thompson complemented each other. Na'ope was the showman, who knew how to gather the talent and make a colorful presentation, while Thompson, the executive director, was a no-nonsense administrator. She was the head of the County Parks and Recreation Department.[30] Although the event did not feature a dance competition until 1971, it soon became the preeminent hula competition in the world. Na'ope and Thompson wanted to bring back the pride in Hawaiian culture and to boost tourism and thereby help the local economy. Over the years, they kept it basically the same with low prices, and the focus was always on hula. Its fame grew worldwide and live television was used for the first time in 1980. It was never meant to be a profitable and revenue-oriented

---

[30] Kumu Leiola worked for the department and was its Summer Supervising Leader at Pahala and Volcano for twelve years.

project, and it shunned corporate sponsorship and government subsidies. Each year the event is sold out, and tickets are difficult to obtain. Hotel reservations have to be made well in advance.

The festival is a well-organized, one-week event. It starts on a Sunday in early April with a canoe race. Canoeing is a traditional Hawaiian activity that experienced a revival during the renaissance. The Polynesians were a seafaring people, and their long voyages were accomplishments worth honoring in this yearly event. The next day, the kumu arrive and have their meetings. This is followed on Tuesday by a meeting of the seven judges, which is the usual complement of judges. Duties of the judges and officials in charge of the competition are demanding. Since the requirements for the competition are extensive and compliance rigorously enforced, the rules on the dance routines and the rules governing costumes and accessories are carefully gone over.

On Wednesday, each dance group is given exactly fifteen minutes to make their presentation. In the first year, nine halau competed, but presently, there are at least thirty. International contestants are represented; for example, Japan sends the winner of their national competition, which is held every two years, to be their official entry. The group presentation is tightly organized, and the day is capped off with a one-hour entertainment. At this time, the royal court is presented, a throwback to the days of the kingdom of Hawai'i.

Thursday is the Miss Aloha Hula contest, an individual competition and the only solo contest in the festival. The following day, the group hula competition begins with *hula kahiko*. From the beginning, *hula kahiko* has been given a major role in the festival and still plays that role today. The festival ends on Saturday with *hula 'auana* competition and the presentation of awards. The program, as outlined, has remained the same year after year. It is instructive to see how the judging is done, for it reveals what factors are considered important in the hula community today. The criteria for judging are as follows:

- *ka'i* (entrance)
- expression
- posture
- hand gestures
- foot and body movements
- chant and song interpretation
- costume authenticity
- adornments
- grooming
- overall performance
- use of Hawaiian language
- *ho'i* (exit)

Based on these criteria, a point system is used to determine the winner, and the difference in scores is usually razor thin and every little nuance counts.

From the beginning of the Merrie Monarch Festival, Kumu Leiola was involved in its planning and preparation, and it was done quietly at her home in Pahala. The work began months in advance and consisted of, among many other things, the preparing of fact sheets and contest songs. At that time, she had become Na'ope's *'alaka'i*, and she was to play an important role in the preparatory work of the festival for seven years.

Kumu Leiola participated as a member of the Johnny Lum Ho's team in the 1971 Merrie Monarch Competition. Her involvement in the team competition became a controversy, and this issue is discussed in Chapter Five. But for Kumu Leiola, the 1971 festival was remembered for another reason. An unusual and frightening incident happened during the competition. While Leiola's dance team was waiting to perform in the dance competition, an official came over and told the dancers to take off their flower leis because the leis were obscuring the colorful costumes. He promptly threw all the leis into the trashcan. The dancers were horrified, for the leis were made with flowers carefully picked and strung together the day before, and these flowers had a sacred meaning.

Leiola excused herself and went to the restroom, and as she entered, an apparition startled her. A lady in white clothing, only visible above the shoulder, abruptly appeared. She was Hawaiian and spoke in her native tongue, warning that discarding a sacred resource—the flower lei—was an affront to the gods. Water suddenly started to gush from the toilet tank. Leiola was petrified and called for help, but when help came, the apparition had already disappeared. The hula competition was stopped and medical aid summoned to help Leiola, who was thoroughly traumatized. 'Iolani Luahine convened a group of kumu to investigate and to discuss what had happened. Someone noticed the flower leis in the trashcan and asked, "Whose flowers are these? These flowers should not be thrown away. It will invoke the wrath of the hula goddess!"

Meanwhile, the toilets were examined and small plastic bags were found in several tanks and inside the bags were Hawaiian salts—red salts from Kaua'i, black salts from the Big Island, and a clump of hair-like substance.[31] No explanation was offered, and the incident itself was never resolved. To this day, Kumu Leiola believes as she has stated, "The apparition appeared because the flower lei, a sacred resource, was dishonored; moreover, internal disputes among the kumu arising from professional jealousies, especially over the use of 'borrowed dancers,' was displeasing to

---

[31] Salt was colored and flavored by mixing with ocherous earth (clay) and was known as *pa'akai 'ula'ula*. See Pukui, *Hawaiian Dictionary*, 297, 517. The hair-like substance probably symbolized *lauoho-o-Pele*, the hair of Pele the volcano goddess. See Pukui, *Hawaiian Dictionary*, 197.

the gods. This was absolutely a warning." As far as is known, the lady in white has not been seen again. It still remains a mystery! After all the commotion, Lum Ho's group, of which Kumu Leiola was a dancer, placed second in the contest. The Merrie Monarch Festival of 1971 was truly a memorable event.

Leiola at Merrie Monarch Festival (1971)
photos by Boone Morrison

While hula competition creates interest and excitement, noncompetitive events can also promote hula and provide participants an opportunity to perform in public. An outstanding example is the Prince Lot Hula Festival, started in 1977 and held in July at Moanalua Gardens just outside Honolulu, but in recent years, it has been held at the historic Iolani Palace grounds. A two-day festival, it is the largest noncompetitive hula event. Named after Lot Kapuaiwa, who became Kamehameha V when he ascended the throne, the festival is sponsored by the Moanalua Gardens Foundation, a nonprofit organization founded in 1970. Hula is the main attraction, but there are food vendors, displays, and demonstrations, making for a colorful event.

The renewed interest in hula and the success of the festivals led to conferences geared for educational and training purposes. They provided opportunities for hula enthusiasts to learn and perfect their performing skills and to interact with other hula practitioners. One unique conference was Ka' Aha Hula 'O Halauaola (KAHOH) World Conference on Hula. It was founded by kumu hula Pualani Kanaka'ole Kanahele (daughter of Edith Kanaka'ole), Leina'ala Kalama-Heine, and Hokulani Holt in 1999 with the support of the Lalakea Foundation. In the post-Renaissance period, nonprofit cultural foundations like the Lalakea Foundation emerged to heighten cultural awareness and participation through educational programs and scholarships and to help preserve Hawaiian culture and tradition. One of the oldest and largest of the foundations is the Edith Kanaka'ole Foundation established in 1990. Its purpose is "to maintain and perpetuate the teachings, beliefs, practices, philosophies and traditions of the late Luka and Edith Kanaka'ole."[32] The Lalakea Foundation is similarly composed of kumu hula and hula practitioners but is more broadly based in its mission statement. It emerged out of the political struggles of Native Hawaiian rights movement, and is involved in protecting environmental resources, those necessary to maintain Hawaiian culture, such as plants, feathers, and other resources used to make hula accessories.

The leadership of KAHOH with the support of the Lalakea Foundation sponsored a series of quadrennial conferences, which met in different islands. The series of islands used followed the story of the goddess Pele and Hi'iaka in their journey across the Hawaiian Islands. The first *'aha* (conference) was held 2001

---

[32] https://www.edithkanakaolefoundation.org/

in Hilo, attended by 1,200 participants with 120 workshops and 93 presenters. Four years later in 2005, it was held in Maui; in 2009, it was in O'ahu, then in Kaua'i in 2014; and finally the fifth and last World Conference returned to Hilo in 2018. Attendance at these conferences has been around 1,500. Besides workshops on hula, sessions were available on costumes, accessories, and the making and playing of instruments, all presented by experts in their respective fields of specialization.

Being away on the mainland for many years, Kumu Leiola has not participated in the Prince Lot Festival or the KAHOH World Conference of Hula, or other conferences and competitions held in Hawai'i. The reasons for not participating are twofold: first, there is the factor of cost. Registration, transportation, housing, and other attended expenses make long-distance trips cost prohibitive. Fund-raising requires time and energy and is an activity Kumu Leiola wants to avoid. Second, there is the heavy responsibility of being in charge of a troupe traveling a long distance with the inevitable accompanying health, safety, and logistical issues. It is a responsibility Kumu Leiola does not look forward to.

For those in Hawai'i, cost may not be a major factor; however, other excuses have been offered for not competing. There are those who differ with the judges on what is most important. They feel the judges are persuaded by the choreography and the flashy appearance. It looks great, and the precision and coordination may be impressive, but what about the meaning of the *mele*? Are the dancers conveying the meaning of the words? Others say it hurts too much to lose; it is not worth the emotional cost. There is the "agony of defeat," with losers crying, not talking at the airport and on the plane, and feeling utterly dejected back in the halau.[33] Kumu Leiola says, "The preparation for the competition takes up too much time, is stressful, and

---

[33] Hopkins, *The Hula*, 135.

takes the joy out of teaching the lessons." Moreover, it creates tension and jealousy between halau.

There have been other festivals and hula conferences, but none have had the staying power of the Merrie Monarch Festival. The Merrie Monarch is unique in that respect; it celebrated its fiftieth anniversary in 2014. The longevity can be accounted for by its insistence on continuously using the same successful formula and not being dependent on business sponsorship and government subsidies. It has, instead, received private donations and volunteer help. As related, there are negatives associated with the Merrie Monarch. It has fostered jealousies, bitter feelings have arisen from the intense competition, and questioning of judges' decisions and standards has occurred. The preparation for the contest is said to have diverted attention from the other vital functions of the halau. But there are more pluses than minuses. There is no denying the role it has played in reviving interest in hula as it has created enthusiasm and excitement. Its reputation has spread worldwide, and more people have been drawn to hula than ever before because of Merrie Monarch. Nevertheless, other conferences and festivals have surfaced, and they have provided needed opportunities for practitioners to perform before a large audience. Practitioners have learned about authentic Hawaiian culture through the seminars, while workshops have given additional information on the making and use of instruments and accessories.

Four decades have passed since the Hawaiian Renaissance. The number of halau has increased, and the number of participants has increased domestically and internationally. Hula is doing particularly well outside of Hawai'i. The first generation kumu of the modern era has passed from the scene. In 1978 and 1979 alone, 'Iolani Luahine, Edith Kanaka'ole, Lokalia Montgomery, Pauline Kekahuna, Pele Puku'i Suganuma, Henry Pa, and Hilo Hattie, all pioneers in some ways, had died. But the second and third generations have taken over the leadership. Traditional *hula kahiko* continue to be perpetuated, and the younger generation has paid homage to it. But there is no denying many divergent styles and innovations are taking place. The Hawaiian Renaissance unleashed a stream of creativity that continues to flow.

"The Hawaiian Renaissance was a time when things were opening up. It was a time to do something and to be someone in hula," says Kumu Leiola. She was in her mid-twenties and was living in Hilo and in Pahala. Except for the Merrie Monarch Festival, she was away from the mainstream of activities. But opportunities opened up in Hilo. She worked at Kapiolani School with the Brownies, girls between the ages of seven and nine, and with the Cub Scouts, a subdivision of the Boys Scouts for boys from eight to ten years of age. She taught all these youngsters, including kindergartners, the hula and various facets of Hawaiian culture—all of these activities were in addition to her work with her halau. It was a time to try new things, and she had the confidence she could handle new challenges.

CHAPTER FIVE

FORMATIVE YEARS

They will spread their wings for a greater flight on the morrow. (Nathaniel B. Emerson)

How a lifetime interest develops is complex and takes many twists and turns. For some individuals, they are able to set their mind to a specific career and are able to achieve it without any deviation, but for most of us, it is not a straightforward path. Family environment plays a prominent role in establishing career interest. Such was the case with Louise Leiola Aquino Galla. She was born in Honolulu in 1944, and "Louise" is her given first name.[34] There were seventeen children in the Aquino family, an astonishing number by today's standard, but in those days, families tended to be large. Life for low-income families in Hawai'i was harsh, and it was a meager existence. Infant mortality was high, and because of the prevalence of communicable diseases, the first few years after birth were considered critical. Of the

---

[34] "Leiola" is her professional or ceremonial name, given to her by Kumu hula George Na'ope, when she graduated and received her *palapala* (diploma). This chapter covers essentially the early and formative periods of Leiola's career before she became a kumu. Therefore, her name "Leiola" is used without the title.

seventeen children, only nine survived past childhood: four girls and five boys. Still, it was a large family.

Leiola's father was Filipino, and her mother was partly Irish and partly Hawaiian. Her mother was from the Landford McKinney Langsi family in Maui, who had several real estate holdings. One aspect of family relationship profoundly affecting Leiola was her step-grandmother's hatred of her mother because of her mixed race. The step-grandmother, who was pure Hawaiian, verbally and physically abused Leiola's mother. As a result, Leiola grew to hate her step-grandmother, and she disliked Hawaiians and their culture. To her way of thinking, all Hawaiians were like her step-grandmother and were prejudiced toward mixed race. This coolness toward Hawaiians and their culture, even the hula, lingered throughout her early childhood. It affected her attitude toward hula, but others in the family, including her father, countered this feeling and encouraged her to take hula lessons. Her mother was not enthusiastic but was supportive. Leiola's grandmother wanted her to take hula lessons and kept telling her to "go to America (mainland) and teach the *haole* (Caucasians) the hula; they will like you."

Through the prodding of the father, all four girls began to take hula lessons at an early age. Leiola was in the middle, age-wise among the girls, and was five years old when she began hula lessons. The girls were in the same halau under the tutelage of Kumu George Na'ope, but they were separated into different lesson groups. Na'ope tended to favor the oldest and youngest sisters, for Na'ope considered Leiola to be tomboyish.

FORMATIVE YEARS

Kumu George Na'ope

It was at this juncture, when Leiola was eight years old, her father made a critical pact with her. He knew Leiola disliked hula, so he said if Leiola would learn hula and become good at it, he would let Leiola join the Police Athletic League, for it was a dream of Leiola to become a star softball pitcher. The promise was made and kept and, indeed, before her father died, he saw how successful Leiola was as a pitcher. In fact, once, he betted on the number of strike-outs she would have, and won. With her sister Ethel, she coached The Rustler's in Hilo, Hawai'i. She played for Continental Flyers (sponsored by Continental Airlines) and traveled to the mainland for games. Later she played in the Christian League, which was less challenging and therefore less stressful. She continued in softball for about thirty years.

However, as fate would have it, her father was even prouder of her because she was the only one in the Aquino family to become a kumu hula. Initially, participation in softball and the ambivalence toward hula caused by her feelings toward her step-grandmother, were factors that slowed the development of her hula career, but due to the promise made to her father, hula gradually became more important and the dislike for hula turned into a passionate love for hula. Such is the irony of life!

Few childhood experiences can be recalled, but certain events can leave an indelible impression on a child's mind. Leiola remembers vividly two incidents having to do with hula. The first incident happened when she was six years old. After a hula performance at a Waikiki hotel, Kumu Na'ope led the troupe of young girls down Beach Walk to the beach next to the Halekulani Hotel. Na'ope told the girls to stand in line on the shore. The girls were wearing *ti*-leaf skirt, their costume for the show, over their short dress. Then they were told to untie the *ti*-leaf skirt and place it in the water. Na'ope explained to the parents this was a dedication ceremony. By placing the *ti*-leaf skirt in the water, they were signifying their dedication to hula. It takes perseverance and determination to be a good dancer.

Another experience that made a lasting impression was the placing of hula musical instruments into a small canoe and setting it out into the ocean. Each dancer had to put their instrument into the canoe. Fortunately for Leiola, her father was skilled in making hula instruments, especially the *ipu*. He had made several but kept the best gourd and let Leiola have one of the others, which became her prize possession. At the beach, the girls were told to put their instruments into the canoe. After Leiola and the girls did this, Kumu Na'ope pushed the loaded canoe out into the water. It was explained—the placing of an instrument of hula into the canoe was like the warrior of old placing his weapon into the canoe.

For a warrior, his tool is his weapon. But for a teacher of hula, the instruments are the tools for teaching hula, and they are everlasting and are available for generations to come. By placing your prized instrument into the canoe, you are making your commitment to becoming a successful dancer. The explanation was given to the parents, for the girls were too young to fully grasp the symbolism. It was later in life when Leiola realized the full meaning of the ritual. For a young dancer to remember clearly these random experiences, shows how powerful rituals can be.

The rituals could become part of the routine, but it depends on the kumu, whether he or she wants to follow the traditions and customs. The rituals could be a means of preparing the students for the training, to motivate them, and to equip them with the proper mindset. There are many types of rituals. A ritual observed by some halau at each session is the recitation by the *haumana* of the password, usually a chant, for entrance into the halau. Once said properly, showing the student has the proper attitude, the kumu hula chants a reply granting admission.[35] Several rituals are associated with the cleansing power of water, so the beach is often used. Students may be asked to find and pick up specific types of leaves or to visit a sacred site and perform a specific set of activities. The short-term purpose of the rituals is to prepare the dancers for the forthcoming lessons or for the competition.

In the early days, the relationship between kumu was loose and informal. Kumu could "borrow" students from another kumu to fulfill their own immediate needs, such as the need for more dancers or to fill a specific void. The kumu who were doing gigs were young men in their late twenties—kumu like George Na'ope, John Pi'ilani Watkins, and George Holokai. They knew each other and were good friends. Na'ope worked for the Parks and Recreation Department of the city, Watkins at Farrington and McKinley High Schools, and Holokai worked for the Kalihi-Palama Cultural and Arts Society. None of them had well-paying

---

[35] Emerson, *Unwritten*, 38–41.

jobs. "They needed rent money, and they were all in the same boat," says Leiola. They had to pay their bills, so side jobs became necessary. The economic circumstances explain why these young men, with their entourage of girl dancers, pursued the entertainment dollar. But a full complement of dancers was not always available because of absenteeism caused by illness or other reasons, and substitutes had to be found. Since the kumu were friends, an informal borrowing of dancers came into play. Later as more kumu entered the scene, borrowing became formal and contractual. Kumu became possessive of their dancers, and as competition between halau intensified, jealousy emerged.

Kumu John Pi'ilani Watkins

Kumu George Holokai

On occasion, kumu would recommend the student seek out a kumu with specialized knowledge about a subject not covered adequately by the halau. For example, if a student wants to learn ancient chants, there are a few kumu who have the expertise, and in most cases, the student would be encouraged to seek the expert kumu. There are regrettably kumu who are not open-minded and are jealous of their "territory" and would not permit their students to go outside the halau. But what is learned from other kumu and the experience of working with them plays an important part in the development of a leader. It is rare, if not impossible, to find a kumu equally versed in all aspects of the hula—dancing, chanting, translation and interpretations, making and playing the instruments, and so forth. Most kumu would readily acknowledge the assistance they received from other kumu. Kumu Leiola could rattle off eight kumu who have significantly affected her career as a hula dancer. Sharing of knowledge and skills is vital to the development of a successful leader.

Kumu Bella Richards, who lived in Kailua, on the windward side of O'ahu, needed help with her hula shows. Kumu Na'ope decided to assist by hiring a driver and a "Rickety Whackety" (a name to remember!) bus to take his students and their parents to the Richards's hula show. The hula show was held twice a month, on Wednesday evenings from 5:30 to 7:30 p.m., and it continued for two to three years. The bus traveled over the Old Pali Road, an engineering wonder of its day, cutting across the Ko'olau Range. It is a narrow, one-lane, winding road, and traffic had to stop to let a large vehicle like a bus to pass through before the traffic on the other side could proceed. Leiola, who was six years old, says, "I will never forget the spooky ride and ghost stories we heard on the way to Auntie Bella's, riding through the unlighted and windy Old Pali Road. It was a really scary experience, but it was worth it, for Aunty Bella taught us *hapa haole hula.* She was cheerful and very sweet and especially loved smiling."

Kumu Bella Richards

As part of their training, the girls in Kumu Na'ope's halau performed in hotel shows, lu'aus, parties, and other public and private events. Leiola recalled dancing when she was nine or ten years old, in the *Lucky's Lu'au* show on KHVH-TV.[36] What was the value of these public performances? They made some money and gave the halau publicity, but for the dancers, it could and was argued that they gave the dancers experience in performing in public, whether in front of a live audience or on television.

Occasionally, there were interactions with Hawaiian musicians. Johnny Almeida, the well-known, blind Hawaiian–Portuguese singer had his studio at the end of the building where Kumu Na'ope's halau was located. After a practice session, Na'ope took a few girls, including Leiola, over to Almeida's studio. The rehearsal began with Almeida singing and Na'ope chanting. The girls in the background decided to call out the few verses of the refrain in jest. Almeida did not seem to object. Surprisingly, it was recorded, so there is a 45 rpm record, where the girls could be heard yelling out the verses! Almeida was noted for singing songs in Hawaiian, and many songs were recorded on 45 rpm; today, they are collector's items.

It was when Leiola was around twelve or thirteen years old, Kumu George Holokai "borrowed" Leiola for about two-and-a-half years to perform in his contracted shows. Again, it was a situation where a critical need existed to have enough dancers to fill the void. During this time, as Leiola observed, her father was helpful in driving her to the various assignments and to Holokai's halau. Leiola had this to say about Holokai: "He was very serious, but he showed me his appreciation by a big hug, and he was very appreciative and humble. He taught me ancient chants. He was a very soft-spoken kumu." Holokai's influence as a dancer, singer,

---

[36] Lucky Luck's real name was Robert Luck, an actor and TV personality of the 1950s, who later was in the *Hawai'i Five-O* TV series.

and musician spanned five decades in Hawai'i. He was a student of Tom Hiona and inherited his studio. He was one of the few, at that time, who focused on traditional *hula kahiko*.

Until 1958, the Aquino family lived in Palolo Evacuation Camp in Honolulu, which was built after the Pearl Harbor attack as wartime housing. This is where Leiola spent most of her childhood. The family moved to Kalihi Valley Housing the following year, but she lived there for only a year before getting married. While at Palolo, Leiola began hula lessons with Kumu George Na'ope, her first and primary hula teacher, a relationship that was to last for thirty-one years (1949–1980). She was not a serious student for the first seven or eight years, viewing hula as recreation, a fun activity. Since her sisters were doing it, as well as her friends, it became the thing to do as a youngster. Besides, her parents and grandmother had encouraged her to go on with the lessons. It took until high school before she began to consider hula somewhat seriously. Over the ensuing years, Leiola said, "The fundamentals of hula came from him (Na'ope). Commitment, style and discipline were taught by this kumu hula." The commitment to hula, however, was not there, for the experience with her step-grandmother had sapped her interest in hula and in things Hawaiian.

In 1956, when Leiola was fourteen years old, her interest in hula was revived. She took an accelerated test and was admitted to Farrington High School. There she met John Pi'ilani Watkins. He was a young kumu in his late twenties and had started teaching hula in 1947. Watkins selected Leiola to be one of the dancers for the May Day program he was hired to do at Farrington. It was a huge program with fifty dancers. May Day programs were held in all the public schools at the beginning of May. It was a program celebrating Hawaiian culture and featuring its music and dances. The program at Farrington was an all-out production. The stage was decorated with flowers and with palm and *ti*-leaves. Hula was a major part of the program, and through this program, thousands of students danced the hula. May Day became a big celebration in Hawai'i. A popular song of the 1940s and 1950s was "May Day is Lei Day in Hawai'i."

Watkins invited Leiola and three other girls to join his regular dancers to do private shows. Leiola considered this a real honor and was delighted a kumu, for the first time, recognized her as a dancer. Technically, she was under the tutelage of Na'ope, but the relationship had become tenuous, and he had given her little recognition. Besides, as discussed, her interest in hula had waned. This was "borrowing," to be sure, but it posed no problem or concern because the dancer was a youngster and was perceived by one side to be unenthusiastic. Furthermore, Watkins and Na'ope were friends. As it turned out, Leiola danced two years for Watkins. Among the places Watkins did shows were Halekoa Hotel and Germaine's Lu'au, a popular tourist attraction. Leiola says

> He (Watkins) was lovable, kind, giving, and so gracious to share with us the dance he taught his students. This is the kumu that changed my thoughts and love for my hula and culture. He never pressured us as dancers, so encouraging, always uplifting us . . . always positive . . . and so forgiving no matter if we forgot our routine. This is the kumu from whom I surely learned to love what I do, be happy, and to be smiling, and to dance the way I believed in; this is how it should be after you are taught the dance. I'm grateful for all the happiness he has shared with me, and that we can smile and love hula while we are learning it.

Up to this point, Leiola had not received much recognition and encouragement from Na'ope. Young dancers need encouragement and support, and this is what Watkins provided. But the most significant influence Watkins had was to change her attitude toward hula and to inspire her to love hula. At age fifteen, Leiola felt good about hula and began to like it; she felt a release from the pressure of uncertainty, and she felt a sense of freedom.

In 1960, Leiola got married at age seventeen. Her first husband, Clarence Pestano, disliked hula and felt hula was taking too much of her time, taking her away from him. As a consequence, she entered a period of hiatus from hula. He worked for Pacific Concrete Products as a supervisor, and the company offered him a position on Moloka'i, the island next to O'ahu. He accepted the offer, so the couple moved to Moloka'i. Their first child, a boy, was born at this time. After two years, the company decided to close operations, and the employees were given the option of going to Honolulu with no guarantee of a job or being laid off. Clarence decided to move to Kapapala Ranch, a small town in the Ka'u District of the Big Island, where his parents lived. He found a job within a month, so the family income was not disrupted. Meanwhile, Kumu Na'ope had moved to Hilo, so Leiola decided to take up hula again and began to dance for him. She was kept busy with the arrival of Sandra Kanela, her second child, at Kapapala Ranch.

Then in 1966, the family moved to Pahala, also in the Ka'u District, not far from Kapapala Ranch. This period marked a turning point in Leiola's hula career—she became a serious hula practitioner. Although still with Na'ope, she became associated with Kumu Edna Aguil, an elementary school teacher. At her halau, Aguil taught only *'auana* or modern hula and did no chants or traditional hula. After Leiola spent a couple of months at the halau, Aguil asked Leiola if she could help teach the supervisor wives group as a teaching assistant. Aguil was cutting back and wanted Leiola to take over completely the halau, but she had to decline because her husband opposed it. In assessing the contribution of Aguil, Leiola says, "Aguil was very pleasant, understanding, never strict or angry as she guided and instructed us in learning hula. This was a small town, and I learned what challenges there are in teaching her ladies class." The importance of Kumu Aguil's guidance is this—she recognized Leiola's abilities and gave her the opportunity to teach. For the first time, Leiola realized she had the skill and talent to be a hula teacher, and this could be her career.

Kumu Edna Aguil

This was a busy time for Leiola in Pahala. Her family grew as she had her third child. In addition to taking care of three children, she found time to manage five halau, namely, Pahala, Na'alehu, Volcano, Pahoa, and Hilo. All five halau were in small towns, except for Hilo. The Hilo halau belonged to Na'ope; he asked Leiola to manage it while he was on an extended trip to Japan. It helped that the towns were all along State Highway 11 (Mamalahoa Highway), but it still took time to commute to these halau. Leiola did this for seven years. It took commitment and perseverance, but she enjoyed teaching the classes.

Mamo Hula Studio (Pahala, 1970s)

Pahoa Hula Studio

In the meantime, Leiola traveled every week from Pahala to Hilo to take lessons from Kumu Leilani Sharpe Mendez. Mendez, herself, had a commute, but her commute was much longer— she flew from Honolulu to Hilo every week to teach over fifty students, including Leiola—what commitment and dedication! Mendez was a prominent hula teacher; she won four times in the Merrie Monarch competition with her dancers from O'ahu. Leiola had this to say about Mendez, "I love everything she gave to hula—strictness, beauty, style, uniqueness, challenges, positiveness, and understanding. She had a heart of gold and had lots of patience seeing dancers grow. . . . she taught me about having strength and to stand for my 'rights' and not be intimidated."

Kumu Leilani Sharpe Mendez

Before he left for a two-month trip to Japan, Kumu Na'ope suggested Leiola "refresh" herself dance-wise and to move a niche up to the next level. He made her his teaching assistant and entrusted her to manage his halau in Hilo. Leiola says, "I honor and proudly say that this is where my strictness comes from, and no matter what, it will be a part of me forever." From Na'ope, she learned how to be a disciplinarian in her teaching.

The next change in residence occurred in 1969 with the move to Hilo. Leiola continued to manage the five halau. She used to travel often the fifty miles to Pahala and Na'alehu from Hilo with Kumu Edith Kanaka'ole. Kanaka'ole was a noted and venerated teacher of ancient and modern hula and was an expert in many facets of Hawaiian culture. She was a legend in the world of hula. Leiola enjoyed talking with Kanaka'ole on these back-and-forth trips. On Saturday after Kanaka'ole was finished with her classes, she would have Luka, her husband, drive her to Leiola's halau, which was nearby. Kanaka'ole would sit for hours without saying a word. Having a master teacher in your classroom will make anyone nervous, but Kanaka'ole never interrupted and never criticized; she just observed. Leiola says, "Just her quietness assured me that I was doing okay. I learned humility, being humble, and having peacefulness when something goes wrong. She and Pualani (her daughter) helped me with my first *'uniki.*" She used to say, "You can do anything you want to. Don't worry about what people say 'cause they're not going to be here to help anyway."

Kumu Edith Kanaka'ole

Polynesian Hula Classes To Begin

Polynesian dance experts from two Hilo hula studios will conduct classes in Ka'u beginning in October.

They are Louise J. Aquino Pestano, formerly of Ka'u and now with Mamo Hula Studio, and Edith Kanakaole, who operates her own studio.

Pestano's instruction in Polynesian dances will begin the first week of October, with classes meeting once a week in Pahala. It is open to persons of all ages. To register, call Pestano at 959-6356.

Kanakaole will conduct her weekly classes in the Naalehu Girl Scout Hall.

Classes will meet each Thursday in three groups. The cost per student each month and times are: ages 8-12, $5.00, 5 p.m.; ages 13-17, $7.00, 6 p.m., and ages 18 and older, $9.00, 7 p.m.

The classes, open to both men and women, will start with ancient numbers, followed by modern hulas.

Persons wishing to sign up or receive more information on the classes in Ka'u are asked to call Olan Carpenter at 929-7181, or Leinaala Enos at 929-9022.

Polynesian hula class with Kanaka'ole
(Hilo, early 1970s)

The Hawaiian Renaissance was underway in the 1970s as Leiola kept busy with the halau. Her marriage was going through rough times with several breakups and attempts at reconciliation. It was a difficult time, but she was determined to be active with her hula dancing. Meanwhile, with Na'ope in Japan, Johnny Lum Ho, a kumu in Hilo, asked Leiola to audition for the competition his group was competing in, and Leiola not realizing the implication, did so and was chosen. Lum Ho claimed he and Na'ope were good friends, and it was OK.

Kumu Johnny Lum Ho

Leiola, with six other girls, now formed a special dance team called "The Kamalani's" (The Chosen Ones). The group performed at several events, and they were paid for each performance. At that time, they were the highest-paid, most-popular group. In the Merrie Monarch Competition, The Kamalani's came in second place in the women's *'auana*. This was the first time the hula contest was held in the Merrie Monarch Festival. From that time on, the hula competition became the main attraction. Soon after this performance, Leiola had to leave the group because she was tied-up with reconciliation attempts to save her marriage.

Not long after Leiola's departure, the group disbanded. It seemed Lum Ho had difficulties with his dancers. Leiola enjoyed the time together with the girls. She says, "I really enjoyed dancing for Johnny and wish we all could understand why he was so unpredictable and negative toward the dancers he had to sing for." When Na'ope returned from Japan and learned about Leiola's involvement with the competition, he was unhappy. After all, Leiola was his assistant teacher and should not be in the contest with another halau. Furthermore, Na'ope's students could not enter the contest because of conflict of interest since Na'ope was co-founder of the festival. Leiola was caught between the two kumu, and it was an awkward and unfortunate situation, and it left bitter feelings. The practice of "borrowed" dancers requires the consent of both parties. Kumu do not want to be taken advantage of and are possessive of their dancers.

In his earlier years, Lum Ho was thought of being a "renegade" kumu. He had no kumu hula mentor, therefore, was not directly under a kumu and had no kumu lineage. He was said to *namunamu* (grumble or complain), a characterization held by dancers in and outside of his halau. Over the years, he mellowed and became less impetuous and argumentative. Lum Ho's halau has frequently entered the Merrie Monarch contest. His halau has produced the most Miss Aloha Hula winners. Since he is from Hilo, he is popular with the local people, and in the Merrie Monarch competition, his group has been a favorite of the audience. His halau is noted for its creativity.

Aside from the friction between Na'ope, Leiola, and Lum Ho, there were other life-changing events in this decade of the 1970s. First, the relationship between Leiola and her husband continued to deteriorate, and finally after the fifth attempt at reconciliation failed, the couple divorced in 1973. Thirteen years of marriage ended, with Leiola awarded custody of the children. Because of the possibility of confrontation, the judge advised her to leave the island. Consequently, she followed the judge's recommendation and left with the children to Honolulu.

The second consequential development came in the midst of marital distress. Leiola had a spiritual awakening. With the guidance of two Christian girl friends in Hilo, she began to study the Bible. Although she grew up in a Catholic family, she had no knowledge of scripture. "The Catholic Vulgate Bible at my parent's house was in Latin and was of no use," says Leiola. The two girls led Leiola in a salvation prayer and helped her to find a personal relationship with Christ. She set aside her burden and accepted Christ as her Savior. A nurturing period began as she attended the Assembly of God church in Pahala. She attended this church that had services in Hawaiian and in English, for five years, and her faith was strengthened.

It was several years later while Leiola was attending the Assembly of God church that she had a dream. One night she began to hear music; she could barely hear it at first—it was so faint. It was coming from the top of the mountain. She walked toward it, going up a series of knolls, grassy hills, all leading to the top of the mountain. It was a beautiful day, with a cloudless blue sky, and the grass was so green. Leiola was drawn to the music and as she continued up the mountain, the music became louder and clearer. After about a half hour, she finally reached the top, and behold in front of her was a large, flat area, like a big stage. The area was covered with a huge tent, and the canopy looked somewhat silky in appearance. And thousands of people were all in groups, and attired in native costumes—Hawaiians, Tahitians, Maori, Fijians, Japanese, Filipinos, Chinese, and other nationalities. Everybody was singing in their own language, "I love You, Lord, and I lift my voice to worship You, Oh, my soul, rejoice! . . ."³⁷ At the back of the tent, Christ appeared. You could only see Him waist high; He was in white, and His hair was radiant, bright, and glowing—a halo surrounded His head. Then Christ spoke, "Go and teach my people to praise and worship me in their songs and dances." Leiola took this as a command, "you go" and "teach my people"—my people meant everyone. The gospel was to be proclaimed by songs and dances in many languages. The music, it turns out, was God's way of calling her. This religious experience was, indeed, a life-altering episode and added a new dimension and perspective and really changed her hula career.

The third development was the drastic changes she had to make in her hula activities. Since she could no longer manage five halau, she gave up three, including the one in Hilo, which belonged to Na'ope and was returned to him. She had remaining the halau in Pahala and the one in the town of Volcano. This decision to hold on to the two halau turned out to be consequential, for shortly afterward, she left Honolulu and returned to Pahala, for she felt the urgent need to actively work with the halau, even though it went against the court's recommendation. As it happened, it was in Pahala that she met Rufino "Dino" Galla. He had worked on Kwajalein Atoll with the US government nuclear testing project as a camera technician and had served with the army in Vietnam. After a courtship of two years, they were married in 1977.

---

[37] At that time Leiola did not know this song. She later learned it was the well-known Christian song, "I Love You, Lord," made famous by Petra, the Christian rock band.

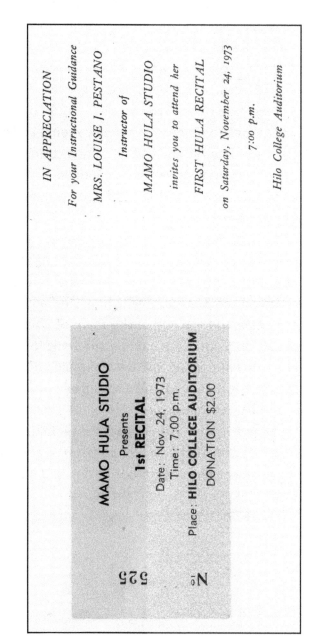

Leiola's recital (1973)

FORMATIVE YEARS

Na'ope's recital (1974)

Galla was always supportive of Leiola's involvement with hula, quite a contrast from her first husband. He was financially independent, had rental properties, and he felt he could find employment of his choosing. There was no pressure to find a high-paying job. In fact, when IBM offered a higher-paying position, he opted to accept a lower paying job at the Ka'u plantation in order to stay in Pahala. With less distraction, Leiola could now concentrate on her hula career. She was still dancing and teaching under Na'ope.

Finally, another event, a tragic one, occurred as the 1970s came to an end. Kumu Na'ope asked Leiola and Dino and Alison Monteban to accompany him to a conference in Honolulu. Alison was a close friend of Leiola. Together, they had studied under Na'ope and both became teaching assistants. They had danced together so often that they developed a close bond. At the conference banquet, Na'ope suddenly asked Leiola and Alison to come to the stage. Then Na'ope officially announced the graduation of Leiola and Alison, and both were awarded their *palapala* (diploma). It came as a total surprise.

Each were asked to do a solo dance, a sort of impromptu command performance before a group of dignitaries that included Dorothy Thompson, co-founder of Merrie Monarch. Leiola and Alison also did a dance together. The dances turned out to be the equivalent of a *ho'ike* in a *'uniki* ceremony. It was not the usual *'uniki*, nevertheless, it was just as effective an announcement to the world of hula that Leiola and Alison were officially graduates; they were now kumu! A few months later, during the 1980 Merrie Monarch Competition, Alison Monteban was killed in a head-on auto accident. It happened at 2:00 a.m., after the last night of the competition, when a drunk driver crossed the median strip and crashed into Alison's car, killing her instantly. It was a total shock to everyone. Leiola was devastated and landed in the hospital. She had to take time off from hula; she needed the break. A few months later, a premature baby girl, Candace Kalei, arrived.

During this period in 1980, Leiola was involved in a pioneering hula instructional program for inmates at the Kulani Prison on the Big Island. This was the first time hula was offered at a prison. Kulani Prison was a minimum-security prison, without fences, for young men who were incarcerated for minor crimes. The project was under the direction of Na'ope, with Leiola working closely with him. New materials were created for the class. For example, chants were written for the inmates in Hawaiian, then translated into English, and finally choreographed into a hula. The inmates danced in the chamber of the State House of Representatives and made such an impression, the legislators passed a bill creating a permanent halau at the Kulani Prison.

It was in 1982, when Dorothy Thompson, head of the County Parks and Recreation Department asked Leiola to do the department's hula program at the Japanese School House at Volcano. She held hula lessons in the basement for two years. Then, she was transferred by the department to Pahala and continued to do hula instructions for ten years until 1994.

The relationship with Kumu Na'ope ended in the latter part of 1980, but before they parted company, he asked Leiola to attend a class on Hawaiian language and history at the Hilo branch of the University of Hawai'i. Leiola said she would attend if he would come along. So they both attended the class taught by Dr. George S. Kanahele and Dr. Malama Solomon. In the long run, it turned out beneficial, for Leiola made the language, history, and culture pertaining to the *mele,* songs and dances, a hallmark of her hula instruction.

Leiola always acknowledged what she had learned from Na'ope. It was never an intimate relationship. Na'ope was too busy to provide the recognition and encouragement desperately needed by a young dancer. But now she was on her own; she could independently run her halau, Hula O' Kaleiola, and to develop her own style, her own trademark. Na'ope's message to her was, "Don't forget what I taught you. You have to watch who you teach!" Why Na'ope would say such a thing sounded strange to Leiola. He had returned from a trip to Japan, having taught hula to the Japanese. Leiola would soon realize what the ramifications were for teaching hula to diverse groups—with the inclusion of new groups comes grave responsibilities—this was his warning to Leiola.

Hula O'Kaleiola
(halau at Pahala, 1991)

As the 1980s decade came to an end, so did the formative years of Leiola's hula career in Hawai'i. She began preparing for the move from the islands to the mainland, but before she left, her sister, Ethelwyne Nahina, presented her with a farewell gift. It was a "song book," which was actually a manual with extensive musical information on hula songs, on the dances itself, and on Hawaiian culture, traditions, and history. It was a source Leiola would consult frequently. A letter enclosed in the song book read, as follows:[38]

HAUOLI LA HANAU

TO MY BELOVED SISTER

---

[38] Ethelwyne Nahina died October 29, 2018. It was her wish to contribute to this book, but failing health prevented her from being interviewed. This letter serves as her contribution.

"LOUISE JANET LEIOLA GALLA"

May this song book bring you much happiness and success in everything you pursue for your "Hula Halau."

You have the characteristics of knowing and practicing our Hawaiian culture and its values. You are truly a Kumu Hula that has inspired many (including me), who have seen (or heard of) your performance.

I am proud for all you have done and what you have accomplished in life, for you and your family. You have overcome all the hardships during your lifetime, many ups and downs, but you have succeeded to live your own life the way you see fit. May the Good Lord continue to give you the strength, knowledge and wisdom, and the power to overcome all obstacles that tries to void your good intentions of doing the good and right things for you and your family.

Nana i ke kuma—Look to the source

Kulia i ka lokahi i ke ola—To strive for harmony in all things

Your beloved sister,
Ethelwyne Nahina

5/21/92

Aquino-Pestano-Galla Hula Family

CHAPTER SIX

FULFILLING THE TASK

"E lawe i ke aʻo a malama, a e ʻoi mau ka naʻauao."
("He who takes his teachings and applies them
increases his knowledge.")
Hawaiian proverb

The formative years from 1950s to late 1980s were times of constant mobility and changes. In the 1990s, however, a new phase began in Kumu Leiola's life and altered her hula career. It was a period when she settled down and found her niche. One day, a neighbor related how she had taken hula lessons in Eugene, Oregon. It seemed odd to Kumu Leiola—why would someone take hula lessons in Eugene? The thought intrigued her so much she got in touch with the hula instructor. It turned out, the female instructor loved hula and had learned *hapa haole hula* from a Hawaiian lady. Although she had been to Hawaiʻi, her knowledge of Hawaiian culture was minimal. Whatever she learned from the Hawaiian lady, she did her best to teach it, but the repertoire was limited, with a few dances repeated over and over.

When she learned of Kumu Leiola's background, she got excited and knew what she was offering was totally inadequate.

She had the financial resources, so an offer was immediately made to pay transportation and a generous compensation if Kumu Leiola would conduct summer workshops. The offer was gladly accepted, and for three consecutive summers, from 1989–91, Kumu Leiola held workshops in Eugene. It proved to be a pleasant experience; in fact, she grew to like Eugene so much, the decision was made to move to Eugene. She found success there and enjoyed her work, but after a little over three years, the asthma attacks became severe and forced her to seek a warm, dry location. Doctors recommended Tucson, Arizona, as an ideal place for those with respiratory problems.

Therefore, in 1996, Dino and Leiola moved to Tucson. Dino found work with the school district, while Kumu Leiola began her hula halua. For the next two decades, she held her halau in eighteen different locations within the city. In seeking a better facility with adequate dancing area, reasonable rent, and a convenient time slot, it meant moving the halau many times. Of course, it was nice having other amenities, such as a restroom, kitchenette, mirror, and storage space. The finding of a suitable location has been a perpetual problem in Tucson. Likewise, finding clients has been a challenge. The clientele has varied over the years. Sometimes, all or a near majority were seniors, most of them retirees. Tucson has a sizable population of retirees and is surrounded by retirement communities, such as Saddlebrook, Rancho Vistoso, and Green Valley.

There are also considerable numbers of military retirees because of the availability of the Base Exchange facilities at Davis-Monthan Air Force Base and a large Veterans Hospital. In conducting hula classes for seniors, a few modifications had to be made, introducing, for example, the less strenuous *hula noho* (sitting hula). Actually, this is an ancient form of hula; early nineteenth-century drawings depicted natives doing the hula in a sitting position. Besides the retirees, college students are another source of clientele. At times, there is an influx of students from the nearby University of Arizona and from the various campuses of Pima Community College. There is, however, one drawback to this particular source—students tend to come and go rather quickly. Finally, military families are another source. Due to duty assignments, several families have spent time in the islands and are interested and familiar with Hawaiian culture, but they, too, are in Tucson for a limited time. These are the major demographic groupings providing members for the halau.

In general, the attendees have been middle age and above. Age level is not a problem, but the transient nature of the population is a serious concern. It affects the development of leaders for the halau. Few individuals have spent sufficient time with the halau to attain the level of teaching assistant. There are those whose limited time with the halau is known beforehand, like students in a degree program, usually about four years, or military personnel with prescribed assignments, usually a two-year rotation. But for the majority of dance students, the time with the halau is unpredictable. People leave for various reasons, such as employment opportunity, job transfer, promotion, and family concerns. Without long-term commitment, the possibility of developing leaders with high degree of dancing and teaching skills is nil. Therefore, commitment and longevity of members present severe challenges for Leiola Hula Halau.

Once Kumu Leiola settled in on the mainland, her skill as a master teacher of hula and a leader of a halau was honed by years of steady experience. Observations of a few advanced students offer insights into what is involved in the make-up of an active kumu. The following sections present a small representative sample of the advanced students on the mainland taught by Kumu Leiola. They are presented in no particular order. The individual comments are arranged into three areas of concern—halau experience, outside performances, and general impressions about the kumu.

SANDI ROSSO

Sandi Rosso served as assistant in Leiola Hula Halau for several years. She came with an extensive background in hula, having taken lessons in Hawai'i for sixteen years. When the Rosso family moved to Tucson, one of the first things Sandi and her husband did was to look for a halau. After surveying the situation, they chose Leiola Hula Halau for its location, safety features, and friendly atmosphere. They were immediately impressed with the strictness of the kumu's teaching style. "While I enjoyed my time at the halau in Hawai'i, I felt the constant pressure of preparing for competition. In Tucson, there wasn't this stressful situation," Sandi says.

"The Tucson halau had a more loving, friendly, and supportive culture. I appreciated Leiola going into the background of songs and dances, and knowing the language, explaining the words of the *mele*," says Sandi. It was more than demonstrating and explaining the body and hand movements. Sandi says, "The chants were an important part of Leiola's program, so time was spent on the chants. For those who were ready, Leiola taught them how to use the instruments." Sandi found "Leiola to be a strict disciplinarian. Once lessons started, it was all business." One day, Leiola got frustrated because the students were not paying attention. Suddenly she slammed the *ipu* gourd so hard on the floor the *ipu* cracked. Sandi muttered, "Oh my gosh!" The other students were aghast. Guess what, Kumu Leiola got their attention!

Regarding outside performances, Sandi related how Kumu Leiola carefully planned and prepared for each engagement. "Rehearsal is held the night before and everyone knew what to do. Leiola was a stickler for details—when to show-up, what to bring, and so on. Her ability to cope with last minute changes—a dancer does not show-up and a quick decision has to be made without getting flustered—was assuring," Sandi says. "Protection of her dancers was a high priority. At a golf club party, a few in the audience had too many drinks and were acting rowdy, so the performance was cut short. There was no hesitation in ending the performance if the audience got out of hand, and if necessary she would refund the money," says Sandi. Usually the audience was receptive and appreciative. Kumu Leiola was good at interacting with the audience and was adept at handling audience participation.

"Although Leiola was a taskmaster, she was compassionate and if something was troubling a student, she took the time to talk and listen to the student. Leiola wanted the students to do their best and sought to motivate them to achieve their goals," says Sandi. According to Sandi, the students respected Leiola and she in turn respected them. Sandi addressed her as "kumu," but students generally called her "auntie." "Leiola was self-effacing; she avoided the limelight and was modest and didn't want to talk about herself. When I served as MC, I made it a point to talk about her unique background. Few knew about her and even her students were not familiar with their teacher's background."

When asked about the kumu's legacy, Sandi replied, "She is a kumu hula, an excellent teacher of hula, but first and foremost, she is a strong Christian woman who loves the Lord and expresses it through the hula." And what has Sandi learned? "Hula is not to be taken lightly because it embodies the Hawaiian culture. Loving hula is a way of sharing the Lord."

KRYSTAL LEHUANANI CLARK

Another student who came with a good knowledge of hula and Hawaiian culture was Krystal Lehuanani Clark. She is of multiethnic background—Filipino, Japanese, Caucasian, and Hawaiian. Currently, she is a school administrator and resides in O'ahu, Hawai'i. Krystal came in contact with Kumu Leiola in an unusual way. She was scheduled to teach hula at Udall Park in Tucson, but at the last minute, had to take a short leave, and Leiola was brought in as an emergency substitute. Upon returning, she joined Leiola Hula Halau and was there for three years and served as teaching assistant.

Quickly she fitted in with the friendly supportive group, and she found Kumu Leiola not too strict and easy to work with. Krystal appreciated the background information on the songs and dances, even the small details on the flowers and plants mentioned in the songs. She took copious notes on the songs and dances, and on the chants. She learned to use the *ipu* and *'ili'ili*, whereas in Hawai'i, after eight years of lessons, she and another sister were never taught to use the instruments, while two other sisters were given the opportunity. It was a blatant example of how kumu sometimes showed their biases and favoritism.

Krystal remarked, "Leiola was detail oriented when it came to the outside performances, carefully planning the program, paying attention to color, costumes, and adornments. . . . Since there was much to do, I assisted with the costumes. As far as I could remember, there were no problems with the audiences, and there were no complaints," Krystal says. There was just appreciative feedback.

Krystal had a close relationship with Kumu Leiola and addressed her by the informal "auntie." "The greatest thing I got from Auntie Leiola was confidence; I learned to acknowledge and appreciate my own talent," she said. Kumu Leiola encouraged Krystal, and she gained self-confidence and was finally able to say to herself, "I'm good!" Krystal believes "Auntie Leiola's legacy is her love of hula. She is proud of hula and wants to share her love of hula with others."

ZELDA AKI PAREDES

A native of Hawai'i, Zelda Aki Paredes, has lived in Tucson for the past dozen years. While in Hawai'i, she had hula lessons, but she took things for granted and did not fully appreciate the dance and culture. When she and her fiancée decided to get married in Tucson, they wanted to have a Hawaiian wedding. There had to be a few compromises; for example, the food was Mexican; but the attire and entertainment was Hawaiian. Her stepmother found a website offering Christian hula; this was precisely the feature they were looking for. The Leiola Hula Halau was contacted, and this is how Zelda met Kumu Leiola. "I was touched by the Christian hula at the wedding; it was a spiritual experience," Zelda says.

When she joined the halau, Zelda was the only Hawaiian, and this surprised her because she was never in a hula group where she was the only native of Hawai'i. "Leiola was strict, stressed the meaning of the hula and explained the background—the history, language, and culture of the dances and music. She did this, in part, by passing out pamphlets and other materials. Leiola was proud of the culture," says Zelda. Zelda was able to play several instruments, some for the first time, and she purchased a few.

Being an advanced student, Zelda was a member of the Performance Group, and she was also asked to do dances at private parties. "Leiola was detailed in her planning and followed a tight schedule," Zelda says. Zelda noticed Kumu Leiola kept track of entries in her folder by using colorful Post-it self-stick notes (adhesive notes); they were reminders, and it is a practice continued to this day, even in the writing of this book!

"I learned humility from Leiola and to be respectful and to listen and not talk over someone," Zelda says. She was impressed with how proud Kumu Leiola was of the Hawaiian culture but, at the same time, showing respect for other cultures. To Zelda, Christian hula is her legacy. "She will be remembered for her love of hula, and how she was always accessible." Zelda recalled, "I once couldn't pay the dues, but Leiola told her not to worry and I could pay later. She said it's not about money. I should be proud of what I'm accomplishing."

SANDY SIEGIENSKI

There are students who have come to Kumu Leiola with no knowledge of hula and only a smattering of information about Hawaiian culture. One such student was Sandy Siegienski of Corvallis, Oregon, where she is a self-employed speech therapist. She said she became interested as a five-year-old, while visiting in Hawai'i, but it was not until she was at the college level, at age twenty-five, when she took hula lessons in Eugene, Oregon from Kumu Leiola. Sandy was her student for two years. "Hula grabs you once you get started," says Sandy. She related, "Leiola had a genuine love for the culture, language, and history, and enjoyed teaching hula. It was important for the students to get the true meaning of the dance and to do it correctly. . . . I studied Hawaiian language, and it was a great help," Sandy says. "Note-taking was required, and we had to write down the meanings of the words and the motions for the entire dance, and there were at times several interpretations, so Leiola explained all of them. Furthermore, Leiola explained the background—the who, why, and where—who created it, why was it done, and where did it take place, all for understanding the story."

Sandy participated in only a few performances. As far as she could recall, there were no real problems; programs were put together with skill. "Leiola kept in touch with the details—colors, costumes, instruments, and so forth—it seemed effortless," Sandy says.

Sandy used the kumu title when speaking with or about Leiola whenever others were around. She said she would "err on the side of formality." "Leiola was respectful and accessible even for haole," Sandy says. Concerning what she learned from Kumu Leiola, Sandy says, "I learned a treasure-trove of Hawaiian culture, and it opened up new areas of inquiry." Her legacy, according to Sandy, "is her love for teaching hula. We should remember how passionate she was. She taught so many about the Hawaiian culture."

LORRAINE GIN

Similar to Sandy Siegienski, Lorraine Gin had no background in hula and little understanding of Hawaiian culture. She is a middle-aged *haole* Chinese and is in the legal field. On a visit to Hawai'i, she became interested in Hawaiian culture. On her computer, Lorraine entered "Tucson hula" and up came, "Leiola Hula Halau." Being a newcomer, she felt a bit intimidated but everyone welcomed her, and Kumu Leiola was especially open to beginners and did not pressure her. "Leiola was not really strict, she pretended to be strict," says Lorraine. Later, Hawaiian language class was started, but she could not take advantage of it, since she was close to leaving Tucson. However, Kumu Leiola translated all Hawaiian words and explained the stories and background of the songs and dances. Lorraine said she got to use the *ipu* and *'uli'uli* and did a bit of chanting.

Gin was impressed with the professionalism of the performances. "High-quality performance reflected the meticulous planning—everyone knew what to do," says Lorraine. She did not experience any negative response from audiences or any complaints, but she did hear how Kumu Leiola handled rowdy audiences.

Kumu Leiola was sort of a "mother figure." Lorraine called her "auntie," but when talking about her, she used the title "kumu." Kumu Leiola did not talk about herself, but Lorraine felt "Leiola had more experience than what she let on. . . . I was inspired and came to love hula because of her," Lorraine says. In Lorraine's estimation, "She is to be remembered for the large number of students she has taught to love hula, and how she has spread this love and knowledge of hula."

PHYLLIS CHATHAM

Phyllis was a newcomer to hula when she joined Leiola Hula Halau. She did not immediately seize the opportunity. After reading an article on Christian hula in the newspaper, she clipped the article and set it aside, for she was too busy at the time working as a school counselor for the Tucson Unified School District. A couple of months after she retired in 2010, she remembered the article about Kumu Leiola and Christian hula. Phyllis had a passing interest in hula since she took a few lessons while she lived in Hawai'i; her stepfather was stationed at Kaneohe Marine Corps Base on O'ahu. She decided to pursue her dormant interest in hula.

"Especially useful was the instructional writing which gave exact steps and served as a guideline," Phyllis says. "Discipline," she said, "varied with the age levels; a younger dancer needs more. . . . Leiola was patient, willing to listen to questions and to repeat instructions. When Leiola had her open-heart surgery, her daughters served as substitutes. Kanela and Kalei were stricter and had less patience," Phyllis says. There was a stark difference in approach, and Phyllis was glad when Kumu Leiola returned. "You were required to take notes, and the Hawaiian language was a step-by-step process, and I found it easier because I speak Spanish and the vowels are similar," says Phyllis. She got to use the instruments, although many dances did not require them.

"For the performances, the goal, of course, was to do well," says Phyllis. "Leiola stressed exact movements and foot placements. Leiola is very detailed. For example, *kahiko* requires ancient costume, and Leiola insists on authenticity. What type of lei differ, with each dance, and it has to be correct." Based on her experience, she says, "Audiences were cordial, respectful, and appreciative, and seniors were most receptive, especially *haole* seniors; maybe it was their wartime experience being stationed or passing through Hawai'i. Audience appreciation made it rewarding."

Phyllis believes students knew a little about their kumu's background, her many years of dancing, and her lineage. "Among the important things I learned from Leiola was to pay attention to details, and to do things correctly, properly, and in order; in other words, don't be sloppy," Phyllis says. In addition, she came to appreciate the history and culture of Hawai'i. "Leiola's legacy is having taught many students to love hula and Hawaiian culture," says Phyllis. "Although I lived in Hawai'i for several years, I didn't know or appreciate the culture. Leiola has passed on knowledge about Hawaiian history and culture to generations of students." Phyllis commented, "You don't appreciate until you realize you could lose it! Leiola's health could mean the end of hula lessons. Now, I appreciate Leiola all the more."[39]

---

[39] Of the seven advanced students interviewed, Phyllis is the only one currently dancing with Kumu Leiola (as of late 2018).

TIANA HAND

Tiana Hand was born and raised in Hawai'i and is of Native American and Japanese ancestry. She is a self-employed graphic designer. Her husband was in the Air Force; consequently, she has lived in many different communities. Presently, she and her family have returned to her native Hawai'i. While growing up in Hawai'i, she did not belong to any halau, but she did take hula lessons at the YWCA. The only hula performances she did were for May Day celebrations at her high school. Therefore, her hula experience was minimal.

When her husband was assigned to Davis-Monthan Air Force Base in Tucson, she looked for any activity relating to Hawai'i. She googled "hula lesson" and "Leiola Hula Halau" appeared on the screen. As Tiana related, "This was a little Hawaiian oasis in the desert!" She found the halau friendly, and she immediately felt at home. "Leiola was understanding of all newcomers and did not pressure us. With established dancers, she was strict and expected and demanded more from them. One thing Leiola was careful not to do was to call out an individual before the group; she didn't embarrass any student," says Tiana. In her teaching, Leiola taught not only the correct techniques, but she went over the meaning of the words in the songs and the background and historical facts of the dances.

As for outside performances, Tiana says, "There were often last-minute changes; it seems inevitable, but Leiola remained calm in the midst of the hustle and bustle of activities. It always turned out good." "Leiola viewed her group as a representative of Hawaiian culture and that's why the performances had to be the best," says Tiana. The performances brought the students closer together. "In the informal gatherings, Leiola talked about her experience, and such sharing brought forth a family circle atmosphere."

Tiana did not expect Christian hula. "I never heard of it," says Tiana. "But once I learned Christian hula, I liked it, and it made Christmas more meaningful." "I remember how much Leiola loved the Hawaiian culture, and how Leiola wanted to preserve it and to share it with everyone"—this, according to Tiana, is her lasting influence.

The comments of advanced students, though phrased in different ways, sounded alike. Each student regarded Kumu Leiola as a strict teacher. Perhaps, at a particular moment, they did not appreciate it, but in retrospect, they recognized the value of having a disciplinarian. There are standards to be met and there should be unwavering focus. It is important to have a teacher who could realize the potential of each student, and who could motivate them to achieve desired goals. Kumu Leiola gave her students confidence. She was their best cheerleader, praising their strengths and acknowledging their accomplishments.

The kumu has to insist on the mastery of techniques and to do them correctly. But hula is not merely techniques. All of the student leaders appreciated Kumu Leiola explaining the words and stories of the dances, songs, and chants. They learned who created it, and why, when, and where it was created. Kumu Leiola was proud of the Hawaiian culture; in fact, the word "proud" was used by almost all of the advanced leaders in describing Kumu Leiola's passion for Hawaiian culture. This pride in Hawaiian culture inspired the student leaders to learn more about the cultural background. This is adding value to the students, something they never expected.

As members of the Performance Group, the advanced leaders appreciated the attention paid to details in the preparation. It enabled everyone to know what to do, thus relieving tension and apprehension. Performing in a group developed a feeling of being a family and built close ties and respect for each other. You learn to trust and lean on one another.

In teaching and working with students, certain qualities are essential to be a successful kumu. All the student leaders pointed out these qualities—the qualities of humility, respectfulness, compassion, and openness. When students are treated with and shown these qualities, the students are appreciative, and they, in turn, are more likely to show these qualities.

There was agreement among the advanced students that Kumu Leiola was imbued with a profound and authentic love for hula and its accompanying culture and tradition; it was her desire to preserve it and to share it with everyone. This is her legacy to the hula community.

It was in Tucson that the above-mentioned advanced students developed all or a major part of their hula skills and attained knowledge of Hawaiian language and culture. What kind of a setting is Tucson for the development of hula? Tucson is not noted as a cosmopolitan city, but it is a university-centered city, and there is a higher degree of cultural awareness—an openness to experience other cultures. With a sizable Hispanic population, the ethnic culture that dominates is the Hispanic culture, for example, mariachi music and folklorico dance are popular. But it seems hula is gaining popularity in Mexico—it has the largest number of halau among foreign countries (see Table 1). Hence, the dominant Hispanic population may not be a detriment.

What other competing factors are there? Besides Leiola Hula Halau, there are three hula studios in Tucson, but these studios are not competitors because their approaches and purposes are different. There is a problem, however, when more than one hula group is invited to participate in an event. It creates competition for visibility in the program and develops jealousy. It is best to have only one hula group represented. But competition among the hula groups has not been a problem. There are enough people in Tucson with interest in hula. The problem is to find them!

To summarize, Kumu Leiola's development as a hula teacher can be delineated into three distinct phases. First, there were the formative years in Honolulu up to age seventeen. She began as a five-year-old student of Kumu George Na'ope but did not show enthusiasm and interest in hula. She treated it as a recreation; although she did experience several interesting happenings, still there was nothing to be serious about. Having mastered fundamental skills, she performed in hula shows as a member of several dance groups, such as those of George Holokai. While in high school, she came under the influence of John Pi'ilani Watkins, who rekindled her interest in hula. She felt appreciated and fully recognized as a dancer.

The second phase was her time on the Big Island, namely her stay in Kapapala Ranch, Pahala, and Hilo. During this period, she was employed for eight years as education assistant by the school district, and in this capacity, she learned how to instruct and work with students. Through her association with several kumu, she was able to transfer these skills to hula instruction. Besides training and working with Na'ope, she learned from Edna Aguil, Edith Kanaka'ole, and Leilani Sharpe Mendez. Not only did she hone her dancing skills, she developed teaching techniques, and learned how to manage halau. In other words, she learned the basic responsibilities of a kumu hula. She gained confidence and now knew she was a professional hula teacher.

The third and final phase began when Kumu Leiola left the islands for the mainland, first going to Eugene, Oregon, and then to Tucson, Arizona. This has been the longest phase, and she has finally found her niche. She is completely on her own and wholly responsible for her halau. Being away from the mainstream of hula activities, forced her to broaden her perspective and to move into new endeavors, such as Christian hula and therapeutic hula, which are described in greater detail in Chapters Seven and Eight. Away from the ocean waves and coconut trees, and missing the ubiquitous "aloha spirit" of the local people, she managed to adopt and adjust new approaches and to move on. This has been her journey—not an easy one—but one with many peaks and valleys. The valleys have been painful. They were times of non-recognition, and even as a kumu, not being accepted by other kumu. The biases and stereotyping on the part of certain leaders have led to discriminatory attitudes, and their ensuing behavior cannot be easily forgotten. These negative experiences could have caused her to misstep, but the peaks made it worthwhile—she sees the journey mainly as a peak-to-peak experience; a journey of hope rather than of despair.

CHAPTER SEVEN

CHRISTIAN HULA AND GLOBALIZATION

Let them praise his name with dancing.
(Psalm 149:3 NIV)

The argument is made that hula is indigenous to Hawai'i, is the life of the Hawaiian people, and should not be used by a non-native religion and in the context of a foreign culture. But part of the Christian community has taken hold of hula, and it seems to be growing in popularity in foreign countries. The affinity, the close relationship between Christianity and hula and with the Hawaiian language, dates back to the early nineteenth century. At that time, a few Native Hawaiians were able to leave the islands for America. They were seeking to escape persecution and wanted a better life. Seven of them studied at a school affiliated with the Divinity School of Yale University. It did not take long before they were converted to Christianity. One of them, Henry Opukaha'ia, was eloquent and pleaded with school officials to send missionaries to Hawai'i to bring the salvation message to his people.

Opukaha'ia did not see his dream fulfilled, for he died before the plan to send missionaries could be carried out. However, four of the Hawaiians were able to be on the first ship carrying missionaries to Hawai'i in 1820. The ship sailed from New England, through the Strait of Magellan, to Hawai'i, taking five months.[40] During this long voyage, the missionaries learned to speak Hawaiian fluently from the four natives and created a Hawaiian alphabet based on the sounds of the spoken language, translating parts of the Bible into the new written Hawaiian language. This was an extraordinary feat, requiring much fortitude and patience. The missionaries brought a printing press, and they were later able to print the Hawaiian Bible. Thousands of Hawaiians learned to read and write their own language, and it helped in the conversion of many to Christianity. Today, vast majority of ethnic Hawaiians profess to be of the Christian faith. The old Hawaiian religion disappeared, and Christianity was absorbed into Hawaiian culture. By all outward appearance, the Hawaiians were Christians, and yet, according to some people, the Hawaiian spiritual qualities remained.

The first missionaries were Congregationalist, but other Protestant denominations began to send their workers. Churches sprang up all over the islands. One of the earliest was Kawaiaha'o Church in Honolulu, built in 1821, under the direction of Rev. Hiram Bingham. It was at churches, such as Kawaiaha'o, where the Hawaiians first heard Western music with its pentatonic musical scale and melody, and they were intrigued by the hymns. The missionaries were delighted to see the natives learning the hymns, but they continued to oppose hula and were against its performance in public. Only a handful saw redeeming features in

---

[40] Orramel Hinckley Gulick, *The Pilgrims of Hawai'i: Their Own Story of Their Pilgrimage from New England and Life Work in the Sandwich Islands, Now Known as Hawai'i* (New York: Fleming H. Revell Company, 1918), 5, 24.

hula, and it took the second generation of missionaries to begin looking seriously at hula.

Missionaries from the Church of Jesus Christ of Latter-day Saints, known as Mormons, soon followed the Protestant missionaries; they began arriving in the 1850s. The Mormon missionaries were more accommodating in their attitude towards hula. They helped to preserve some aspects of hula, particularly the chanting. A few native converts to Mormonism became proficient in hula, and one of the earliest Mormon kumu was Pua Ha'aheo, who was noted for his powerful chanting, and for his role as a dancing instructor. His students included Kau'i Zuttermeister, Sally Wood Naluwai, and Ma'iki Aiu Lake; they all became well-known kumu.

Mormon kumu, who developed along different genealogical lines were Mary Kawena Pukui, Edith Kanaka'ole, 'Iolani Luahine, Keake Kanahele, and Eleanor Hiram Hoke. They became pioneer kumu who had significant roles in the development of hula. A large Mormon temple was built at La'ie and a branch of Brigham Young University, called Church College of Hawai'i, was later established. It was at La'ie that the Mormons helped create the Polynesian Cultural Center in 1963, which today is a prominent tourist attraction.

For Protestants, Catholics, Mormons, and other believers who became interested in hula and wanted to learn the dances, a series of critical questions had to be confronted. First, was the question of the *kuahu* (altar), which in ancient times was in every halau. Elaborate rituals and prayers were performed before the altar, and there were distinct rules and conduct and prescribed rules on the construction and decoration of the altar. Emerson observed, "In every halau stood the *kuahu,* or altar, as the visible temporary abode of the deity, whose presence was at once the inspiration of the performance and the luck-bringer of the enterprise—a rustic frame embowered in greenery."[41] Any defilement and violation of the rules had to be cleansed by prayers and by sprinkling with salt water and turmeric. Another way to be cleansed of defilement was to bathe in the ocean. But these practices were onerous to Christians.

If the kumu is a Christian, he or she simply dispensed with the *kuahu,* and with the elimination of the altar, the accompanying rituals, rules, and practices disappeared. For the student, the only option is to abstain or excuse oneself from the activities, or if that is not allowed, then the student has to leave the halau. But as the ancient Hawaiian religion began to fade, the *kuahu* were gradually eliminated and the rules and rituals reduced, relaxed, and often were unobserved. Today, by and large, majority of halau have no *kuahu.* Whatever rituals and practices remaining are viewed as a tradition rather than a medium for venerating the gods.

The second question is what to do with certain practices in the halau. By tradition, the hula session is opened or closed with *pule* (prayer). In ancient times, *pule* were said at hula performances, but with the decline of the Hawaiian religion, the practice today is more a traditional ritual rather than a religious act. Since Kumu Leiola is a Christian, she avoids misunderstanding by making it clear to her students, *pule* said in her halau is *pule* to *Akua* (Christian God). It is optional, and students may abstain. There are practices that are clearly offensive; one example would be the *'ailolo,* ceremonial meal, where the food had been offered to the gods and goddesses. These halau practices with their accompanying problems could be avoided by not participating—by abstaining from the rituals. Practically speaking, it does not affect the performance of the group, and it does not cause confusion or disruption, so abstinence is acceptable.

---

[41] Emerson, *Unwritten,* 15–16.

Finally, many of the chants, *mele,* and dances honor Pele and Laka. How do Christians reconcile their love for hula, knowing some chants and *mele* are honoring other gods? In situations where abstention is permitted, being allowed to abstain would be the best solution. But for the dances, it may be difficult to substitute another set, especially for *hula kahiko,* where not participating would affect group performance. Therefore, abstention may not be allowed; in which case, a decision has to be made by the Christian. Many Christians resolve the dilemma by making a distinction between honoring/respecting and worshiping. A Christian can respect Hawaiian culture, its dance, music, chants, and *mele* but not worship their gods and goddesses. Then, the honoring of their deities is only a symbolic gesture. It makes it possible to embrace cultural diversity and makes for tolerance by allowing for choices while not compromising one's religious beliefs. Cynics may say this is "mental gymnastics," but for the true believer, they have to resolve this question and come to an unambiguous stance.

A few testimonies illustrate how individuals handled these questions about Christian beliefs and ancient Hawaiian rituals and practices. George Na'ope, talked about his kumu, Mama Fujii: "Mama Fujii taught me only *kahiko* but since she was a Christian, she only talked about the *kapu* (taboos) during my training. She would also teach us sitting dances and the *oli,* but there would be no *kuahu.* There would only be Christian prayers before and after we danced."[42] Na'ope recognized the Christian practices and was not troubled by them. Many years later, when Kumu Leiola was his assistant, she had a long conversation with him on Christian beliefs and how his worries could be taken away. Na'ope listened attentively but did not respond.

---

[42] Itagaki. *Nana,* 112.

A devout Catholic and mentor of many outstanding kumu hula, Ma'iki Aiu Lake commented, "I learned that the *kahiko* could be performed without all the rituals. I didn't have to be afraid, and I didn't have to compromise my Christian faith."[43] Liffie K. Johansen Pratt, hula teacher for over twenty years, wrote: "My parents were both pastors in a Hawaiian Christian Church in Keaukaha, Hawai'i, and for years I've had spiritual battles going on within me. I was taught both the old Hawaiian religion and the Christian religion, and I've tried to come to terms with this dual religion all my life. Today I am a born-again Christian and an ordained Evangelist, and I've re-dedicated my halau as a Christian hula halau. Although I no longer do the chants of our *kupuna* (ancestors), my God Almighty has been giving me some beautiful chants and songs for my halau. The songs and *mele* are different, but the hula is still being perpetuated."[44]

Another kumu, Kevin Michael K. Mahoe, who heads the Christian Hula Academy said, "We were never taught the ancient ways because we were baptized and raised as Christians. In my heart I felt I could not rightfully worship Jehovah and at the same time participate in the offering of prayer chants to Laka, Pele, or Hopoe.[45] The hula that I do today, the interpretation, the motions are all inspired by God."[46] Taking a broader view, Kumu Edith Kanaka'ole, a Mormon, said the message of her Hawaiian culture and the message of the gospel were similar. "We must live and love unselfishly, because that's the only way we enlarge

---

[43] Itagaki, 84.

[44] Itagaki, 121.

[45] "A dancer who Pele turned into a balancing rock at Puna, Hawai'i." See Pukui. *Hawaiian Dictionary*, 82.

[46] Itagaki, *Nana*, 100.

our souls." Her often-repeated saying was, "Ulu a'e ke welina a ke aloha" ("the growth of love is the essence within the soul").[47]

Since Kumu Leiola is a Christian, her halau does not have a *kuahu*. She does not follow any of the rites and practices relating to the ancient deities. Before anyone becomes a member of her halau, they are informed about her religious beliefs and are told there will be opening prayer. As previously mentioned, prayer is optional, and no one is required to participate. Kumu Leiola is careful not to impose her religious beliefs on anyone. She explains why there will be Christian hula in the repertoire; in lieu of dances dedicated to Pele and Laka, Christian hula is offered. The practice session at Leiola Hula Halau begins and ends with Christian hula. Kumu Leiola believes Christian hula sets the proper mood and conveys the message that practicing hula is enjoyable but a serious business. When performing in public, she mentions there will be Christian hula in the program. "There are mixed reactions to Christian hula," says Kumu Leiola. "Some think we shouldn't dance about God or sing about Him. If we are performing, and someone requests that we not do Christian hula, we don't."

It is not known when the Christian hula movement began, but by the time of the Hawaiian Renaissance in the 1970s, Christian groups in churches were probably practicing the hula. In the beginning, it was amorphously organized and done informally by church ladies. It slowly became a part of the church's ministry, but not part of the worship service. And this is how it remains today in most churches. There are a few churches where "worship hula" is a part of the worship service; dancing is considered an expression of worship and is allow in the service, but this is not the norm. In somewhat of a concession, in

---

[47] Hopkins, *Hula,* 104.

1998, the Catholic Bishop of the Honolulu Diocese allowed hula during Mass.

In most churches, the hula ministry is geared for teaching the hula and performing only at church social events. For example, the Saddleback Church in Southern California, a mega-church, has a hula ministry called Ka 'Ohana Ho'Onani. There are three classes for women of different age levels, meeting during the weekdays, and this ministry is considered part of the outreach program. Sometimes church groups combine their resources. Seven nondenominational church groups in the San Diego area have formed a regional organization; they meet to exchange ideas, share resources, and to socialize. Today, churches in Hawai'i, the mainland, and in Japan have hula classes and perform the dances as part of the church's ministry. In Japan, Christian hula is commonly known as "gospel hula." Whether in America, Japan, or any other places where Christian hula is performed, hula is viewed by Christians as a gift from God. Through hula, God is worshiped, praising and glorifying His name. According to Christian respondents, when dancing the hula, they feel the presence of God and are given spiritual sustenance.

Leiola dancing Christian hula
Japanese Christian Church of Tucson

What is the process by which Christian hula comes about? Kumu Leiola explained it this way: "The hula is based on a Christian hymn, which has been translated into Hawaiian. Frequently, the hymn has already been recorded and available as a CD. It can be in Hawaiian or in both Hawaiian and English. Then the hymn is choreographed; this is the part that is time-consuming. There is a limited number of Christian hula video available that could be used to see what has been done, but they are not to be copied, for they are usually lacking in quality." She tells her students to look for the Hawaiian word *Akua* (Christian God) to find a Christian song. The music often captivates the students, and they want to purchase their own personal copy but are told they cannot have the one used in the halau because it is the property of the kumu and are, therefore, *kapu* (prohibited) for outside use. Students could go online and purchase another version of the Christian song.

The key to producing successful Christian hula according to Kumu Leiola is prayer. "I pray about the selection of the song, its translation, its choreography, and even the costume. It's no problem when the dancers are all Caucasian women because of their fair skin, but with a mixture of Asian and Polynesian dancers, there is variation in skin color, and this affects the color coordination of the costume." Her prayer covers all phases in the creation of Christian hula.

Leiola dancing Christian hula
First Southern Baptist Church, Tucson, Arizona

Hymns in both Hawaiian and English have a long history, going back to the early missionaries. The lyrics of the old hymns were translated into Hawaiian, but sometimes only the tunes of the hymns were borrowed and new lyrics were written in Hawaiian and in English. The classic song "Hawai'i Aloha" was written by Lorenzo Lyons, an early missionary. He was fluent in Hawaiian and wrote the lyrics in both Hawaiian and English, using the tune of the hymn "I Left It All with Jesus."[48] One can imagine on Sunday morning at the Kawaiaha'o Church, hearing the nostalgic strains: *"E Hawai'i e ku'u one hanau e, ku'u home kulaiwi nei"* ("Oh, Hawai'i, my own birthplace, my own native home")—opening words of "Hawai'i Aloha"—it must have resonated and stirred the hearts of the natives! Today, these hymns are readily available and are gradually been put into dance forms, providing resources for the Christian hula movement.

GLOBALIZATION

Christian hula can be viewed as part of the globalization process, for it has been exported to and established in other countries. It would be instructive to see how Christian hula took hold in a country. Here, however, we are concern with the globalization of hula, the spread of all types of hula in a foreign country. As shown in Table 1, hula has expanded worldwide with Mexico, Japan, and Canada having the most halau. Japan has been selected as an example of a country where hula grew exponentially. Within the Pacific Rim, with Hawai'i in the center, mainland US in the east, and Japan in the west, the advancement in communication and transportation has accelerated the globalization of hula.

---

[48] "Hawai'i Aloha" was one of two songs proposed for Hawai'i's national anthem. The State Legislature selected "Hawai'i Pono'i."

Japanese interest in hula began in the 1920s and 1930s. This pre-World War II interest was primarily due to the popularity of Hawaiian music and Hollywood movies glamorizing hula. The war interrupted the Hawaiian craze, but it picked up again in the immediate postwar period of the 1950s. Here, the *Nisei* (Japanese Americans) musicians from Hawai'i, who performed in Japan, contributed to the popularity of Hawaiian music. Several *Nisei* were soldiers or civilian employees with the American occupation forces in Japan, which lasted until 1952.

In the ensuing decades, Hawaiian music remained popular in Japan, but for hula, sustained interest did not occur until the early 1980s. Hula began to be taught at private community schools, known as "cultural centers." The sponsors were major department stores and newspaper companies, and this was not unusual, for these companies were already sponsors of baseball, soccer, and other sport teams. Hula classes provided a good image for the companies and made for excellent public relations.

Middle-aged housewives were targeted for the classes, since they had leisure time and money to participate because this was the boom period of the Japanese economy. The hula dance was advertised as a low-stress form of exercise. Japanese women were health conscious and into physical fitness, and dance was viewed as a form of exercise and pleasure. The dance form as exercise was already familiar to Japanese women; they were acquainted with ballroom dancing and Western folk dance. The participants were almost exclusively women, not surprising, since even in America, hula was considered for a long time as a female dance form.

Three of the favored Hawaiian songs were "Blue Hawai'i" and "On a Little Bamboo Bridge," both of the 1930s, and "Beyond the Reef" of the late 1940s and early 1950s. In line with the popular Hawaiian music, the Japanese ladies were attracted to *hapa haole* and *'auana* dances. *Hula kahiko* was neither seen nor heard. It did not matter whether the songs were in Japanese or English; the ladies knew the tunes and understood the lyrics, thus overcoming the language barrier. Moreover, the songs had a nostalgic effect—it felt wonderful to dance to these old goodies.

The 1990s brought forth a new, younger generation. Before the bubble economy burst, many young Japanese were able to travel to Hawai'i. They had the money, and the yen exchange was excellent. Consequently, droves of young people came as tourists, and many became interested in Hawaiian culture. When they returned to Japan, they noticed the difference in the hula being taught and what they had seen in Hawai'i. They noticed the hula at home had become "Japanized" and had not kept up with contemporary hula. What Japanese students sought was authenticity. Some made special trips to Hawai'i and studied with Hawaiian kumu.

If they could afford it, Japanese students in the art world always sought the best teachers. Therefore, they sought prominent kumu in Hawai'i. In Japanese society, studying with a renowned teacher gave you greater prestige and status, and when you became a teacher of hula, pedigree is important; it meant you could attract more students. For the kumu in Hawai'i, it was also a good deal. After all, having a sister halau in Japan became a status symbol and besides, it was more income; Japanese students were willing to pay high fees—they wanted the best. As a new generation of Japanese kumu emerged, they moved away from the cultural centers and opened their own halau. In addition to *hapa haole hula* and *'auana*, they offered *hula kahiko* and began using the ancient percussion instruments. Some classes geared themselves for participation in hula competitions held in Hawai'i. In fact, every two years, an all-Japan hula competition is held, and the winner becomes Japan's official hula team for the Merrie Monarch.

Today, there are approximately 500,000 hula dancers in Japan. There is no official count, so only an estimate can be given, but if Japan has a half-million hula dancers, it would be more than Hawai'i! There is enough of an audience for two Japanese hula magazines, the *Hula Le'a* (The Joy of Hula) and the *Sutekina Hula Style* (Gorgeous Hula Style), to exist. Of the two, *Hula Le'a* is the more prominent and established magazine. In general, Japanese hula lessons are more expensive than what is charged in America. For some Japanese kumu, it is a profitable business. Usually the Japanese kumu instructs only the advanced students. The assistant teacher covers the beginner classes, and they are held at the cultural centers or at gyms, since facilities are often scarce. Presently, to become a kumu requires a long period of training. At the end, the candidate receives a certificate in a formal ceremony—there is, of course, a fee charged for the certificate. To top it off, the candidate is given a ceremonial Hawaiian name!

Japanese kumu often have a close relationship with Hawaiian kumu. Many of them visit Hawai'i several times a year. Hawaiian kumu, in turn, are invited to Japan to hold workshops. Kumu who have gone to Japan include: Kent Ghirard, George Na'ope, Johnny Lum Ho, Alan Barcarse, Ray Fonseca, Sonny Ching, Frank Hewitt, Rich Pedrina, Nalani Keale, Shane "Maka" Herrod, Aloha Dalire, and some others. Kent Ghirard and his group was probably the first to tour Japan back in 1955.[49] But the kumu who paved the way was Na'ope. Starting in the 1970s, he was the first kumu to broadly teach hula to the Japanese. One of his students, who became a kumu, had about three thousand students, and she brought a small contingent of dancers and musicians year after year to the Merrie Monarch Festival to perform as invited

---

[49] Itagaki, *Nana*, 46.

guests at the Wednesday night *ho'ike* presentation. By the 1990s, conditions began to change dramatically.

Workshops in Japan that used to attract about one hundred students now drew about two thousand.[50] What accounts for the huge turnout? As previously discussed, there were the socioeconomic factors. There was a spike in the popularity of hula from the early 1980s to mid-1990s because of the booming economy. Women had more money, leisure time, and travel opportunities, and the role of women in the family had changed. But what is it about hula itself that attracts the Japanese?

Japanese respondents gave several reasons for taking hula lessons, and the responses were, not surprisingly, similar to those of Americans. Reasons cited by Japanese women included exercise, weight loss, stress release, hobby, and so on. They even mentioned the healing process for taking up hula. But for serious Japanese dancers, the answer cited by Kumu Frank Hewitt probably captured best the Japanese attraction for hula—they simply loved and valued the beauty of the dance.[51] The Japanese women said they did not quite understand the words of the dance at the beginning, but as they studied and practiced the dances, they came to a deeper knowledge of the world around them and came to understand their inner feelings; so the beauty of the dance is more than simply its surface qualities.

Christian hula is the platform from which the gospel message reaches out to new audiences, and to reach new followers for Christ. The globalization process has allowed the popularity of hula to cut across political, racial, language, and cultural barriers. Sometimes Christian hula and globalization came together. Such was the case with the Japanese Evangelical Missionary Society

---

[50] Eloise Agular, "Japan Hooked on Hula and the 'Ukulele." *Honolulu Advertiser,* July 11, 2005.

[51] Agular (2005).

(JEMS) Gospel Hula Mission trip in 2010. Besides performing in churches, the group danced in various public venues, providing the Christian message in the context of Hawaiian culture. Hula has proven to be a powerful medium, whether to share the gospel or to disseminate Hawaiian culture. Hula can no longer just be tribal; it has to be global.

CHAPTER EIGHT

THERAPEUTIC HULA

> Observe your dog; if he's fat,
> You're not getting enough exercise.
> (Evan Esar)

Hula, as previously discussed, has been exported to other countries and has thrived in diverse cultural settings, and has been used by Christians to praise and glorify God. In this chapter, we explore the expansion of hula into another realm: its use for therapeutic purposes.

The human body has amazing strength and flexibility but can only endure a limited amount of hardship. Too much physical work can damage the body. On the other hand, complete inactivity is bad for our body and could lead to health problems. Our body is designed to require physical challenges. If you have a dog and the dog is fat, you need to get up and take the dog for a walk. There is another facet to consider. We are not fashioned to endure great amount of mental and emotional stress. Stress could impair our physical capacities and even lead to depression. It seems tension could be lessened by physical exercise, so exercise is essential.

You often hear the phrase "I need to exercise." Exercise is not a strict discipline, and we are free to do what we want; it is a God-given freedom, but it can become a moral imperative to act. You wear a Fitbit, you exercise; in other words, you *do* something. Dancing is widely recognized and accepted as a form of exercise and is beneficial for our health. It does not have to be strenuous, high-impact aerobic dance, such as zumba or the rapid hip-shaking Tahitian dance. Even modest exercise has significant health benefits, and as it turns out, most dances are sedate, low-impact activity that eliminates jumping and pounding, thus decreasing stress on the joints. Low-impact dance programs are now regular offerings in fitness centers, YWCA, YMCA, health clubs, and other private and public establishments; classes include low-impact aerobics, folk dances, ballroom dances, line dances, belly dances, and, of course, hula.

Some halau offer hula as a weight-loss program, but for the most part, this is done to bring in additional revenue. Weight loss is only a concomitant, a minor side effect of hula dancing. Leiola Hula Halau does not have weight-loss classes. A few students in Leiola Hula Halau do cite weight loss as one of the reasons for taking lessons, but in most cases, it is not the principal reason.

Hula requires the use of several muscles, especially of the arms and legs, so warm-up is necessary, even if you exercise regularly. Warming-up muscles before the lesson prevents injuries. Warm muscles are more pliable and less likely to tear than cold muscles, which contracts sluggishly and can be injured. Muscle tone is important to consider, hence Kumu Leiola requires warm-up exercises. Certain muscles around the shoulder, arms, and knees are important in dancing and need to be strengthened.

Middle-age women often find it difficult to maintain the bent-knee posture required in hula. They need special exercises to strengthen their knees and legs. For some seniors, balance is a challenge, and this needs to be worked on. The kumu has to be perceptive as to the exercise needs of the students. Kumu Leiola uses slow-stepping Christian hula as the beginning warm-up exercise. Christian music itself is modulated at a slower pace. The class session ends with another Christian hula; it is excellent for winding down. The dancer should feel good after the class session.

Therapeutic hula has been of great help, particularly with three groups of people: seniors of retirement age; to a limited extent, professionals; and people with disabilities. Therapeutic hula is meant to help and treat those with physical and mental challenges and disorders, and those who want release from stress. It is not a cure but serves to take care of those with these challenges. More than physical need is involved—it is working with the mental and emotional states of the individuals. Kumu Leiola has worked extensively with seniors of retirement age throughout her career. At times, she has worked with individual seniors with handicaps or with group of handicapped seniors.

One day in Eugene, Oregon, a well-dressed lady in her sixties approached Kumu Leiola and said she was an early-retired teacher and wanted to learn hula.[52] She asked for an appointment. Kumu Leiola asked her to come to the basement of the library where the halau was located, but the lady insisted on going to Leiola's home. Kumu Leiola thought this was strange but consented. When they met, the lady hesitantly asked if she could have private hula lessons. Kumu Leiola said it could be arranged but would be expensive, since it would be hourly rate. The lady still acted hesitantly and slowly lifted her dress to reveal wooden prostheses on both legs. In those days, prostheses had long straps down to the heels and were crude, not what we have today.

---

[52] For privacy reason, the name of the lady is not revealed. Today she is in her nineties and resides in Eugene, Oregon.

The lady was embarrassed, but Kumu Leiola noticed how easily she moved around. Kumu's reply was, "No problem, we could begin the lessons as soon as possible." The initial lesson was private at the halau as requested, but when it ended, eight ladies came in for their group hula class. She observed the class session, and the ladies seemed to be having fun and seemed friendly. After the second private lesson, she decided to join the ladies' group. She went on to become an active member of the halau, and the crowning event was the halau recital, where she did three dances. She did them beautifully and nobody knew she wore prostheses! Later, Kumu Leiola received a letter from her, thanking Leiola for the hula lessons and how she had gained confidence. She had always felt inadequate, that she was not like the others. Now she had achieved something she thought she could never do; she had the power to accomplish whatever she wants. For Kumu Leiola, this gaining of self-confidence, the attitude of "I can do it," is more precious than the mastery of the hula steps and movements. One's life is literally turned around.

Sometimes a large group of seniors with disabilities is involved. In Eugene, she had over thirty wheelchair-bound seniors, sixty-five and over in age, gathered in a community center. She had them do *hula noho* (sitting hula) using castanets and split-bamboo sticks. With these instruments, the seniors kept time with the rhythm of the Hawaiian music, and they thoroughly enjoyed the exercise. They said it was a relief to get away from their usual boring exercise; doing hula with instruments was fun! This class was held for two-and-half years until Kumu Leiola had to leave Eugene because of her asthma.

In a community center in Pahala on the Big Island, Kumu Leiola met with a large group of elderly Japanese. They were seventy or more in age, but for their age, they were surprisingly energetic. She bartered hula lessons for martial arts and *bon' odori* (festival dance) lessons.[53] No money was involved, just an exchange of services. Two Japanese songs were choreographed into hula movements. The Japanese seniors enjoyed the hula; it was something new, and they said it was fun and good exercise. Kumu Leiola was amazed by their enthusiastic and energetic response.

Professionals are another group seeking relief through hula. Included in this group are doctors, lawyers, and other professionals, who have found the website of Leiola Hula Halua, and are looking for private lessons to relieve stress. Because of privacy concerns, their names cannot be revealed. Kumu Leiola says, "One of the first question they ask is what kind of hula do you teach?" They tend to view hula as a "hip-moving" dance, but she is quick to point out she teaches traditional Hawaiian hula, not the glamorized versions. These professionals are looking for relief from the strain on their bodies, both mental and physical, from long hours in the office or clinic. Once hula is tried, they find it is a way to relieve stress, and is an enjoyable activity.

A couple of doctors on an exchange program came to Tucson from Prescott and Flagstaff, Arizona, cities at least three-hour drive from Tucson. They took hula lessons and found it effective in reducing stress and enjoyed their sessions so much, they wanted to continue their lessons when they returned to their homes in the northern cities. They paid Kumu Leiola to come to their homes. "I'm a traveling kumu, and I like working with interesting people," Leiola says. Private lessons can be expensive, so the clientele is limited to those with higher income; though small in number, this form of therapeutic hula is an important component of the services provided by Kumu Leiola.

---

[53] The secularized bon dances are performed annually in mid-July to mid-August as part of the Bon Festival celebrating the arrival and then the departure of the ancestor spirits.

A rewarding experience has been the work with teenagers, seventeen to eighteen years of age and young adults in their early twenties, all with some form of disabilities or disorders. In Tucson, Kumu Leiola has worked with Mirasol Recovery Centers. Mirasol provides integrative treatment for eating disorders, substance abuse, autism, and related autism spectrum disorders (ASD). Their approach is to respect the individual client and to focus on the root causes of the problem rather than on the symptoms. The aim is for the individual to develop new ways of communicating and coping.

Kumu Leiola came in contact with Mirasol through one of its employees, Carol Magee. Sometimes contacts are made on the slimmest of encounters, and the story is worth telling. Carol took hula lessons while living in Pahoa on the Big Island of Hawai'i from 1995 to 1999. Once she left Hawai'i, she did not continue hula lessons for the next twenty or more years. One day while wandering through a Tucson museum devoted to Southwestern arts, she came upon a room surprisingly filled with Hawaiian art objects. On the table was a photo album of a kumu with her dancers. Carol asked the museum director about this kumu and was given Kumu Leiola's name and phone number. This is how Carol came to meet Kumu Leiola and became a member of her halau. Carol introduced Kumu Leiola to the owner of Mirasol; the owner visited the halau and observed a few classes and was so impressed, she hired Kumu Leiola to teach hula at Mirasol.

Kumu Leiola developed hula programs for teenagers and young adults with the volunteer assistance of Candace, her daughter, and with Carol's help. The teens were taught separately from the young adults. Besides the hula lessons, they were taught the tradition and history of hula, *lei* making, chanting, and the use of instruments. The results were surprising, and staff members were delighted with the outcome. The young people embraced and thoroughly enjoyed the sessions. The classes became a highlight for the teens, and when the lessons were not held for about a month, the teenagers were disappointed and wanted the classes to resume as soon as possible. Following are their candid comments:

> I really enjoy hula because it teaches me that exercise can be really fun, and I don't have to do it perfectly. I'm allowed to just be gentle with myself. (Marge—young adult)

> Hula is fun and empowering because it is difficult to accomplish, and exciting when I get the steps right. Thank you! I look forward to dancing each week with you all! (Adele—teenager)

> There are so many things that get in the way of enjoyment for me, especially when it involves any kind of movement. It's a struggle with body image, perfectionism, insecurity, my inner critic. But with hula, it's different. I love the ease and gentleness of it. I love that it's storytelling. I love that it's new and different, and the sense of accomplishment when I get through the song. I love the smiling . . . the (hula) movement, not so I can perfect it, not so I can lose weight, not to prove myself, but for the genuine fun of it. (Maya—young adult)

> Hula is lots of fun. It always makes me smile and laugh. (Toni—young adult)

> I have been in dance for about five years— dancing ballet, modern, jazz, hip-hop, and so

> on. But I had never learned to hula dance. This class is an amazing inspiration that I can carry on for future dances. Not only is it interesting to learn new dances, but it also helps me by being a coping skill. I can use hula dancing to ease my pain and turn it into fun. As a bonus, I now get the chance to learn and sing the Hawaiian language. (Ashton—teenager)

> Before I started my treatment at Mirasol, I've never heard of hula classes, so since the first day, I was surprised and interested in it. From the first class, I fell in love with the concept as well as the kindness of the instructors. I also realized how fun hula is and how happy it makes me feel. Hula helps me with my depression because it makes me forget about my problems . . . hula is a tool for expressing my feelings, as well as learn about the Hawaiian culture and spend time with my wonderful friends and peers. (Alex—teenager)

Alex also wrote a letter when Kumu Leiola had to be away for five weeks.

> I'm writing this letter with the purpose of letting you know what happened in the five weeks you couldn't come (emoji with sad face). First of all . . . I missed you so much, your energy in the room changed ours, your beautiful smile, positivism, and your loving nature makes us feel like at home. Those five weeks without hula weren't great (emoji with sad face). Hula for me is a way of expression and a way to be nourished with

happiness; I'm so grateful for being part of this beautiful hula family. Thank you so much for everything. I hope I can still be part of this, as well as how hula is part of my heart too. With love, Alex (emoji with smiling face)

As the following comments show, it is more than dancing. The teachers, fellow dancers, and the surroundings have to be supportive. Hawaiian music and culture as a whole, all play an important part.

Hula is more than dancing and singing, it tells a story, history, future, and love. The hula dances have more power than other types of music like, "JB," and so on. When I watch my friends do it, it makes me feel calm. The music is not stressful. It's peaceful. I am grateful to be able to be taught, and to see what it truly means. When Leiola was gone for about a month, all of us were sad that she was not here. And for me when she was not able to come, I felt something was missing . . . just seeing everybody have a good time makes me feel that I can also feel happy as well . . . I can say from meeting Leiola, I see music in a different way and how music can tell a story . . . a *lei* is such a great gift to ever get, and all the love is put into making it so beautiful. The instruments are so beautiful, and the sounds they made were so fascinating to me . . . so that's what I learned. (Julie—teenager)

Finally, a letter summing up the feelings of the young people; they love hula and look forward to the lessons.

It wasn't the same the few weeks when you weren't here. I missed hula a lot. I felt a little sad when we didn't have hula because I loved it so much. Every week I look forward to doing hula with you. We sang the songs a few times when you were gone because we all missed it so much. I am really glad that you are back now and that we get to learn so much more from you. You are such an amazing teacher, and I love all the time I get to spend with you. I am so grateful to have gotten the opportunity to learn about hula and Hawai'i; it makes me want to go there again. (Dahlia—teenager)

The responses of the teenagers and young adults point out two factors critical for the success of any hula class. First, the lessons have to be fun, that is, they have to be enjoyable; clients must thoroughly like it. Second, the clients have to be made comfortable by creating enough space for each individual. They must feel totally at ease with the surroundings—the instructor and the fellow dancers have to be supportive and encouraging. Exercising with friends makes it pleasurable. These two factors, enjoyment and feeling comfortable, motivate clients to attend the classes and to be eager to participate and to learn. Moreover, their interest is expanded; they learn about Hawaiian culture and tradition, they learn to appreciate Hawaiian music, and they even learn some Hawaiian words. Carol commented, "Leiola always made the classes fun with lots of laughter . . . she encouraged these teens and young adults clients to feel good about themselves and gave them courage to try new things."

Observation of the teacher provides another perspective on the effect the program had on the students. Kumu Leiola kept notes on the progress of the program. Herewith are her notes on the case of Eve, a thirteen-year-old autistic girl with an eating disorder:

> For four months, every Tuesday at 11:00 a.m., I taught hula lessons to Eve. At times, she was not in the mood for anything. Her attitude was bad, ugly, and bitter. I had to ignore her and went on teaching other students. Then, suddenly, she asked me in a begging voice if she could recite the words of the chant, which I was doing the drumming with the *ipu heke* (double gourd drum). I was surprised she knew every word and had the proper cadence. Then, she danced and recited the song with her *kala'au* (rhythm sticks). This was a total surprise—absolutely no mistakes. This song has four verses and is repeated twice with entrance and exit *kahalo* (a dance step). Of all the years I have worked with special education students, I have never come across a child like this. She taught me what wonders our hula can do. Eve has difficulty speaking and writing, but she can read the words and recite them just like a Native Hawaiian. For me, the result has been a blessing.

The young people at Mirasol with their different forms of disabilities and disorders—eating, substance abuse, autism, and related autism spectrum disorders—represent diverse needs. There are no known cures for most disorders, and in most cases, a long period of therapy is necessary. What would help meet the needs? Medication is only part of the answer. When a student asked Kumu Leiola if she could get off a prescribed drug, Leiola told her to go to her doctor who had prescribed the drug. Kumu Leiola was careful not to give medical advice.

What Kumu Leiola did was to meet the diverse needs by having an inclusive program of hula classes accessible to everyone and to have a welcoming learning environment. The attention was on the individual rather than on their impairment. Hula became a mode by which students could express themselves. It helped with the psychological and spiritual needs, which in turn, impacted the behavioral responses. Hula, of course, was not a cure, but it temporarily relieved the stress and helped bring about incremental changes in attitudes and behavior patterns. The hula lessons helped improve social interactions and the verbal and nonverbal communication skills. Staff members considered this a significant development. Just the smiles on the clients' faces showed their spirits were uplifted.

What is reported here is not based on scientific analyses, for there are no clinical studies specifically focused on the therapeutic value of hula. What we have reported are anecdotal observations. Nevertheless, there are studies on the effectiveness of specific types of exercise, including dances, on neurological disorders; exercise slows progression of diseases and reduces symptoms.[54] Moreover, music therapy has been shown to have therapeutic effects on communication capabilities, social skills, emotional development, and on stress and depression. Since music and dance are closely related, by extrapolation, it could be said with confidence, hula could have similar effects. As seen by the above responses of the participants, significant changes had occurred in the attitudes and behavior of these young hula dancers.

---

[54] Dr. Becky Farley has shown in her research the effectiveness of certain types of exercise on reducing the symptoms and slowing the progression of Parkinson's disease. See becky@pwr4life.org

In looking back at the program, the bottom line for Kumu Leiola, Candace, and Carol was the response of the young people. When the young participants eagerly looked forward to the classes and were thrilled to dance the hula, or surprisingly demonstrated their skills even though impaired by emotional disorders, this was all the psychic reward Kumu Leiola and her assistants wanted and needed—it made their effort eminently worthwhile. "It was a terrific experience for me!" shared Carol.

Kumu Leiola can sympathize with those afflicted with physical or substance abuses and with those having low self-esteem and confidence. She, herself, went through the experience of being a victim, so she understands what is needed to overcome these mental afflictions. During her childhood, she witnessed or experienced abuse first-hand, both verbal and physical and even sexual. She witnessed the abuse of her sisters and her mother, and there were two suicides within the family. Alcoholism and drug abuse were recurring problems in her dysfunctional family. She learned early on, turning to alcohol and drugs were not the answer to relieve the pressures of life. She was pulled down by humiliation and self-doubt, but what caused her to pick herself up? Ironically, "What I didn't initially appreciate (hula), turned out to be healing for me," Kumu Leiola said. "No matter what you go through, drugs and alcohol are not the answer to your problem. Hula was therapeutic and helped to make me a better person." Hula and her Christian faith kept her on the right path, so she could continue the journey.

EPILOGUE

"I ulu no ka lala i ke kumu."
("The branches grow because of the trunk.")

"Ho'omoe wai kahi ke kao'o."
("Let all travel together like water flowing in one direction.")
(Hawaiian proverbs)

Hula is a series of contradictions. In order for hula to grow, it has to change, but change means moving away from old practices and losing parts of the past traditions. Some people want change to take place quickly, so there would be dynamic growth; whereas others want minimal change, with slow, evolutionary steps, so there will be stability. But it does not have to be starkly black and white. Change can simultaneously have positive benefits as well as negative consequences. Contradictions could be antagonistic, where clashes occur with harmful effects, or it could be symbiotic with mutual benefits. For instance, *hula kahiko* has different contradictions. When the change occurs organically, that is, from within, where change takes place incrementally, then the contradiction between the old and the new tends to be symbiotic. On the other hand, if the change in *hula kahiko* is imposed abruptly by outside forces, for example, the new instrumentation effect on the cadence of the chant, the contradiction between old and new tends to be antagonistic.

Of all the contradictions, probably the most controversial has been the clash between form and substance. By form, we mean the emphasis on outward appearance, fast body movements, eye-catching costumes, and all the flashiness audiences prefer and even favored by competition judges. By substance, we mean the emphasis on the words, the meaning of the *mele*, and how accurately and effectively the story has been translated and told by the dancers. This contradiction has caused heated discussions.

Besides the contradictions, some practices are said to be anachronistic—they do not belong to present time. These rituals are found in halau and at times performed in outside ceremonies. An example would be the purification rites. Of course, these rituals are offshoots of the old Hawaiian religion and mythology. Adherents argue these practices are part of Hawaiian tradition and culture and should be maintained. The elimination of the rituals would damage the integrity of hula—rituals are part and parcel of hula. Furthermore, supporters say rituals are essential for instilling discipline. Most hula followers, however, say these rituals have lost their meaning and are no longer relevant. It comes down to keeping one foot in the past and valuing highly the history and tradition, and at the same time, with the other foot, stepping into the future by excluding old practices and adopting new procedures. How do you accomplish this balancing act? That is the challenge.

Certain problems in hula today were revealed by the journey of Kumu Leiola. How these problems are resolved will determine to a large degree the direction and future of hula.

HAWAIIAN LANGUAGE

A majority of hula teachers have only a rudimentary knowledge of the language. The language skill level is still low, although it has vastly improved from the abysmal conditions of pre-renaissance days. The lack of language skills leads to misinterpretation and loss of interpretation. Many meanings are lost, especially *kaona* (hidden meaning) found in the chants and *mele*. Subtlety is lost, that is, the ability to discern or understand fine distinctions in meaning. Dancers tend to learn and teach by rote, and little attention is paid to the meaning of words. It is mechanically spouting the words, and this has led to the emphasis on body movements at the expense of the meaning of the words. This is not a recent problem. Emerson commented in the early 1900s, "The average hula dancer of modern times shows great ignorance of the *mele* he recites, and this is true even of the kumu hula. His work too often is largely perfunctory, a matter of sound and form, without appeal to the intellect."[55] Today, kumu recognize the problem, and there is consensus among them that language is critical and will definitely affect the future of hula.

COMPETITION

In the old days, there were few halau, and with a wide-open free market, there was little competition for students. Also, there were opportunities to perform for free or for money. Kumu used to temporarily borrow dancers from other kumu when they needed additional help to fulfill contracted engagements. But, as the number of halau increased and competition developed, the practice of borrowing dancers diminished, and borrowing

---

[55] Emerson, *Unwritten*, 28.

became formal and contractual; this was a departure from the informal verbal agreements.

Competition was heightened by the appearance of hula contests. Several halau made the preparation for competitions one of their principal focuses. Winning became the goal—it would bring fame and fortune—it would immensely enhance the prestige of the halau. One halau has entered over thirty consecutive Merrie Monarch Competitions, but there are negative consequences, for the preparations are always time-consuming and stressful. Although winning brings joy and happiness, losing brings cynicism, despair, and disillusionment. The losers would claim the system was rigged and biased, and criticize the rules and even the criteria used in judging the contest. Competition does create interest and enthusiasm and draws a large crowd, but it does have its drawbacks.

POPULARIZATION

Whenever hula is geared to please the populace, there is a tendency to glamorize it and to make it showy and alluring. This emphasis on the superficial, the outward appearance, comes at the expense of the inner meanings, the story of the hula. The tradition and history of the dance is neglected or ignored. The subtle movements are dropped or, even worse, exaggerated to please audiences.

The popularity of hula leads to increasing commercialization. Hula is tied in with tourism and the entertainment industry—this becomes its dominant activity. Today, hula itself has become a business industry. With the increase in halau and in class enrollment, the income from lesson fees has become substantial, involving many thousands of dollars. To this could be added the money spent on instruments, CDs, DVDs, costumes, accessories, manuals, and other paraphernalia connected with hula and Hawaiian culture. It amounts to a large sum of money. Furthermore, participants in competitions spend sizable amount of money for registration, travel, hotel, food, and other related expenses. Hence, the popularization and commercialization of hula has resulted in taking considerable time and resources away from the original intent of just dancing hula for its sheer pleasure or for sharing it with an intimate gathering of friends.

Despite its negative consequences, popularization is needed to expand interest in hula, to promote growth, and to improve the financial conditions of dance organizations. It is possible to popularize hula and still maintain high-quality standards, and at the same time remain true to Hawaiian tradition and history. In 1995, the first dramatic epic hula, *Holo Mai Pele* (Pele Travels) was performed. Created and choreographed by Pualani Kanaka'ole Kanahele and her sister Nalani Kanaka'ole, it is a three-hour hula epic put on by their halau, Halau O Kekuhi. It is considered to be the first hula opera, combining classical theater form with ancient chants and hula. The dancers in stunning costumes perform against a backdrop of huge slide images of Hawaiian sceneries. The performances were widely acclaimed. It was taped and was aired on the PBS series "Great Performances" in 2001. The production has also gone abroad, touring Japan and Mexico in 2006.

The next major production was *Hanau Ka Moku* (An Island Is Born), co-produced by Halau O Kekuhi and the modern dance troupe Tau Dance Company, premiering in 2002. It included hula and contemporary dances and used both ancient and newly composed chants. The performances attracted large audiences, and the interest was so high, the production went on tour, covering O'ahu, the Big Island, Maui, and several cities in California.

Along the line of large stage productions was the well-known works of Kumu Patrick Makuakane of San Francisco. They included productions such as *The Natives Are Restless* (1998), which told of the early history of hula; the silver anniversary production, *Twenty-Five Years of Hula;* and *Kumulipo* (Source of Darkness), honoring the Hawaiian creation chant.[56]

The above examples of large stage productions, with striking costumes and the use of multimedia techniques, attracted large attendance, and the performances were critically acclaimed. There were those who were bothered by the juxtaposing of the old and the new—ancient chants with modern music, *hula kahiko* with contemporary dance—but the detractors would have to admit, it was artfully combined. The stories were faithfully and accurately told, and what was impressive was how the views and feelings of the Native Hawaiians, their practices, traditions, and history were portrayed.

APPRENTICESHIP

There are other concerns, but one final challenge is apprenticeship. In the past, it required many years of training to be recognized as an accomplished dancer or master teacher. The title of kumu was earned after a long period of apprenticeship, and it was the master teacher who decided when it was time to confer the title. The requirement of a long period of training is not unique to hula, for in most of the artistic fields, and in the traditional crafts, long period of tutelage is necessary. It is more than the mastery of skills; the attainment of mental discipline and the drive for perfectionism necessitates extended period of training, which is labor-intensive and time-intensive. But this is antithetical to the demands of modern society.

We live in a hurry-up society. Fast food, fast service, and instant gratification are expected and demanded. Everyone is in a rush. Few young people today want to endure a long period

---

[56] Simon, "A Tale," 51, 53.

of training. Apprenticeship often means a lack of recognition and the carrying out of endless menial tasks. Moreover, with a mobile population, few people are staying at the same locale for an extended period. Before, it was possible to find an individual who was willing and able to accept discipleship and to be with the kumu for a decade or more. Not so today. Whatever the reasons, the longevity of students has lessened, consequently, the pool of skilled and ambitious leaders has diminished.

Counter to the problem of apprenticeship has been the rise of new generations of leaders. With the passing of the pioneer kumu, new generations of energetic and forward-looking leaders have emerged. An example is the Kanaka'ole family. Edith Kanaka'ole, the pioneer matriarch, died in 1979. Daughters Pualani and Nalani inherited her halau and continued teaching the distinctive 'aiha'a style and the old chants and have reaffirmed their commitment to the old traditions. Pualani is the president of the Edith Kanala'ole Foundation, and Nalani is the artistic director. In 2007, Pualani gave up her position in the halau to her daughters, Kekuhi and Huihui Kanahele-Mossman, who along with Nalani became the kumu hula of the halau. Presently, the halau is under the direction of Nalani and Huihui. This multigenerational lineage of the Kanaka'ole family is unique. There are other families with generations of leaders, but they are not as extensive. In the Kanaka'ole family, the basic thrust, values, and traditions have been largely followed by the succeeding generations. There are innovations in performance techniques and use of technology and media by the younger leaders, but on the whole, there is remarkable continuity.

Kumu Leiola has two daughters who are kumu. Sandra Kanela Pestano Alatan, the oldest, has a halau on the Big Island. The younger daughter, Candace Kaleimamo'owahinekapu Galla, is a professor at the University of British Columbia and specializes in the revitalization of indigenous languages. The Hawaiian language serves as a model of a revitalized language. Both girls were trained in hula from early childhood and are steeped in the hula tradition. But there are differences between the two girls and their mother in their thinking and approach to hula, resulting from variations in personalities, training background, and experiences.

The following generalizations are presented here for comparison purposes. First, on the halau, Kumu Leiola presently favors the use of rented private facilities and is open to various features. Kanela, on the other hand, has primarily relied on church facilities and is not demanding in the kinds of features offered. For Candace, the facilities need to have specific niceties, the more the better, and it needs to be orderly and organized; she is fastidious. Therefore, the halau would look different—Candace's halau would be elaborately organized, Kanela's would be user-friendly and homespun, and Kumu Leiola's would be in between the two extremes. The biggest difference is in the teaching style. Although a disciplinarian, Kumu Leiola is patient and understanding of the abilities of students and is accessible to students. Kanela and Candace are also strict but are more demanding and not as patient and are less prone to understand and have empathy for individual needs. Kanela tends to be laid-back in her relationships with students; whereas Candace is cognizant of each student's health, interests, and their affairs—in other words, she knows each student's background.

Christian hula and therapeutic hula are personal interests and prerogatives of Kumu Leiola. Kanela teaches Christian hula, and this is expected, for her halau is in a church. Kanela is not directly involved with therapeutic hula but has worked with wheelchair students. Candace helped as a volunteer at Mirosal, and the youngsters were especially excited when she visually explained the songs and dances by using a computer.

EPILOGUE

A final note on the generational difference—the use of technology clearly differentiate the younger from the older generation. Both Kanela, and especially Candace, use the latest computer equipment, techniques, and programs. Candace skyped Hawaiian language classes to her mother's hula classes in Tucson. This was probably the first time such innovative approach has been used. Occasionally, the mother has to ask her daughters for help, but isn't this the case in all families, where the kids are better equipped and knowledgeable about computers than their parents?

For all the differences, the degree of consensus is striking. All three, Kumu Leiola and her daughters, agree on the use of the instruments, the need to motivate the students, the necessity for detailed planning in the preparation and carrying out of performances, and in the handling of the audience. They are similar in being community-minded and in their outreach to the public. And most important, they are in agreement on the importance of the Hawaiian language, and in the direction hula is taking. Finally, they are optimistic about the future of hula.

Although the younger generation leaders may have different priorities, emphases, and approaches, there is agreement on the basic purposes and functions of the halau. Multigenerational leaders are actively carrying out the task of teaching and disseminating the knowledge and skills relating to hula. Hula is in good hands. The younger generation has committed to preserving the old traditions and to use it as a framework to enhance our understanding of contemporary developments. After all, the things that don't change give a meaning and a perspective to the many things that do.

Kumu Leiola tends to view hula from a traditional perspective, but she is willing to change and to adopt innovations. Her views on the fundamental challenges facing hula can be summarized. First, she is a firm believer in the need to develop language skills;

the knowledge and use of the Hawaiian language is absolutely essential. Second, she believes competition is overemphasized, and while acknowledging the necessity to increase visibility of hula and to broaden its appeal, intense competition does invites negative consequences of complaints, jealousies, and a drain on resources. Why can't there be more noncompetitive hula festivals? Third, Kumu Leiola recognizes the need to popularize and commercialize hula for economic reasons and to widen its support, but she is critical of the glamour and glitz, and she has some reservations about the movement to make it an extravaganza. Finally, she is particularly concerned about the nature of apprenticeship. In her case, apprenticeship was needlessly extended. The mentor-disciple relationship has become anachronistic. Yes, it takes years to master the skills to be a teacher of hula, but the process is arbitrary and depends wholly on the whim of the kumu hula. Ingrained biases, stereotypes, and possessive attitudes lead to discriminatory practices, not acceptable in contemporary society.

In the preface, we made a statement that needs clarification. We said, "Hula is the artistic language of Hawai'i, but hula is also the artistic language of the world." It is often said hula is the life of Hawai'i, the soul of Hawai'i, and the heartbeat of Hawai'i—the metaphors differ but the message is the same, hula is, indeed, the essence of Hawaiian culture, and is therefore, "the artistic language of Hawai'i." This fundamental feature of hula cannot be changed. It cannot be duplicated or transposed; it remains ineffably Hawaiian. This is why Hollywood-type hula and Tahitian dances are not traditional Hawaiian hula and are not copies of it. It is important to recognize the uniqueness of hula and its language. To Kumu Leiola, ʻolelo (language) and hula are the blessings of God and for this, we give thanks and praises to *Akua* (Christian God). What God has given is unique, and that is why it can never be copied. This is the exclusiveness of hula.

In contrast, the phrase, "hula is the artistic language of the world," denotes hula as a dance medium; it is a means or mode of artistic expression. Therefore, we can speak of hula as a medium used by other approaches, as in Christian hula and therapeutic hula, and the expansion of hula outside of Hawai'i, as in the globalization of hula. In Kumu Leiola's dream of music coming down from the mountain, Christ commanded her to go to all the people with the good news of the gospel using songs and dances, and this meant doing it with different languages and using different approaches. Hula is being used to reach everyone. This is the inclusiveness of hula. So, we have "hula as the artistic language of Hawai'i"—its exclusiveness, and we have ""hula as the artistic language of the world,"—its inclusiveness.

Changes will continually take place, but hula should prosper, as long as there is large number of followers who enjoy dancing. There is something contagious about hula—you want to do it, and you want to show it to others. Individuals do not take up hula for financial gain or public approval; they do hula for pleasure and to learn about the dances and its culture. At the end of this journey, we return to the inclusive mantra "Come dance with us," to which *Kumu* Leiola would add, "and to thank Him for this opportunity to glorify and praise Him!"

GLOSSARY

Some words have several meanings. Only the definitions relating to the text have been selected. The definitions are mostly based on Pukui and Elbert, *Hawaiian Dictionary*.rev. ed., 1986.

'aha   conference.

'ai ha'a   a style of hula with bended knees, low-posture and done vigorously.

ai kahiko   in the ancient style.

'ailolo   ceremonial meal.

Akua   Christian God.

'alaka'i   teaching assistant.

ali'i   chief; ruling elite.

'auana   modern hula.

ha'a   early dance with bent knees; later called hula.

halau   meeting place where hula is taught.

haole   white person; Caucasian; foreign.

hapa haole   half white, half Hawaiian; mixed Native Hawaiian.

hapa haole hula   hula danced to modern Hawaiian songs in Hawaiian or English.

haumana   student.

heiau   temple; shrine; place of worship.

ho'i   a parting chant to which hula dancers dance as they leave the audience.

ho'ike   to show; the dances in graduation exercise.

ho'opa'a   greater experienced dancer; chanter.

hula 'auana;   see 'auana.

hula hapa haole;   see hapa haole hula.

hula kahiko;   see kahiko.

hula ku'i   interpretive hula mixing the traditional with the modern, introduced during the reign of Kalakaua.

hula nema nema   name of hula performed for Kalakaua's coronation.

hula noho   sitting hula.

hula 'olapa;   see 'olapa.

'ili'ili   pebbles used in dances.

ipu   percussion gourd.

ipu heke   double-sized gourd.

kahako   macron, a diacritical mark placed above a vowel to aid in proper pronunciation.

kahiko   ancient hula.

kahuna   priest.

ka'i   entrance; to come dancing out before an audience.

kala'au   rhythm sticks.

kane hula   men's hula.

kaona   hidden meaning.

kapa   tapa made from bark.

kapu   sacred or holy; taboo; prohibited.

keiki   children.

kiho'alu   slack key; the strings are picked individually and are not chorded.

kuahu   altar.

kuleana   responsibility.

kumu   teacher.

kumu hula   head of halau.

kupuna   ancestor.

lei hulu   feather lei.

maile   a native twining shrub with shiny fragrant leaves and used for decorations and leis.

maka'ainana   commoners.

malo   male's loincloth.

mele   songs and poetry.

mu'umu'u   loose-fitting gown.

namunamu   grumble; complain.

'ohana   family; kin group.

'ohana nui   extended family; clan.

okina   glottal stop.

olapa   dancer or dances of lowest level.

'olelo   language.

GLOSSARY

oli   chanting.

pahu   drum.

pa'i   beating or drumming.

palapala   diploma.

pa'u   woman's skirt; sarong.

pikake   jasmine with small, white, fragrant flowers.

pu'ili   split-bamboo rattle.

pule   prayer.

'uli'uli   feathered gourd rattle.

'uniki   graduation exercise.

BIBLIOGRAPHY

This list is meant to guide readers to the relevant sources cited in the text and to suggest further reading.

Agular, Eloise. "Japan Hooked on Hula and the 'Ukulele." *Honolulu Advertiser,* July 11, 2005.

Barrere, Dorothy B., Mary Kawena Pukui, and Marion Kelly. *Hula: Historical Perspectives.* Honolulu: Bishop Museum Press, 1980.

Emerson, Nathaniel B. *Unwritten Literature of Hawai'i: The Sacred Songs of the Hula.* Rutland: Charles E. Tuttle, 1965.

Gulick, Orramel Hinckley. *The Pilgrims of Hawai'i: Their Own Story of Their Pilgrimage from New England and Life Work in the Sandwich Islands, Now Known as Hawai'i.* New York: Fleming H. Revell Company, 1918.

Hale, Constance. "Keeping Step: Auntie Mae Kamamalu Klein is a Living Link Between Hula Past and Present." *Hana Hou!* 20, no. 6 (December 2017/January 2018).

Hopkins, Jerry. *The Hula.* Hong Kong: Apa Productions, 1982.

Itagaki, Jan M. and Lovina Lependu, eds. *Nana I Na Loea Hula (Look to the Hula Resources)* vol. I. Honolulu: Edward Enterprises, 1984.

Itagaki, Jan M. and Lovina Lependu, eds. *Nana I Na Loea Hula (Look to the Hula Resources)* vol. II. Honolulu: Everbest Printing Company, 1997.

Pukui, Mary Kawena. *'Olelo No'eau: Hawaiian Proverbs and Poetical Sayings.* Honolulu: Bishop Museum Press, 1983.

Pukui, Mary Kawena and Samuel H. Elbert. *Hawaiian Dictionary.* Revised and Enlarged Edition. Honolulu: University of Hawai'i Press, 1986.

Simon, Liza. "A Tale of Two Kumu." *Hana Hou!* 14, no. 1 (February/March 2011).

Stillman, Amy Ku'uleialoha. "On the Kuleana of a Kumu Hula." https://amykstillman.wordpress.com (2011).

Stillman, Amy Ku'uleialoha. "Printed Sources About Hawaiian Music and Hula." https://amykstillman.wordpress.com

Stagner, Ishmael. *Kumu Hula: Roots and Branches.* Honolulu: Island Heritage Publishing, 2011.

Young, Peter T. "Hula—How the Missionaries Felt." imagesofoldhawaii.com/hula-pahu (December 8, 2013).

ABOUT THE AUTHORS

Leiola Aquino Galla

Of Filipino, Irish, and Hawaiian ancestry, she has taught hula for over forty-five years on the Big Island of Hawai'i and in Eugene, Oregon, and Tucson, Arizona. She was a student of the pioneer hula master, George Na'ope, and has been associated with and influenced by some of the foremost instructors in the world of hula. A participant in the renaissance of hula, she has been an innovator in Christian hula and therapeutic hula.

Minoru Yanagihashi

Born and raised in Hawai'i, he is a second-generation Japanese American. His educational background includes: BA, University of Hawaii at Manoa; MLS, University of Washington; MA, University of California, Berkeley; and PhD, University of Michigan. He has taught at several colleges and universities, and his interest ranges from Japanese history and government to the role of Japanese Americans in Hawai'i and on the mainland.

CPSIA information can be obtained
at www.ICGtesting.com
Printed in the USA
FSHW010631231219
65143FS